"A tool, a key and ar
forgiveness is and much
advice to experience ar
leads us to a very profound relationship with our God, the God of
mercy and infinite love. These pages are filled with the Word of God
and illustrated with real-life experiences. I pray that this book touch
and "unlock" the lives of many men and women and help them find
freedom and abundant new life!"

GÉRALD C. CARDINAL LACROIX
Archbishop of Québec, Primate of Canada

"There is no freedom in unforgiveness. In *Forgiveness Is Key*, Angèle
Regnier is a blessed companion on a journey to the center of
Christianity: living completely in surrender to the Trinity, in and
with and through Love that transforms."

KATHRYN JEAN LOPEZ
senior fellow, National Review Institute and co-author of
How to Defend the Faith without Raising Your Voice

"When forgiving seems impossible, and when asking forgiveness seems
unpalatable, this delightful book will help you reclaim God's perspective:
Forgiveness is possible, necessary, and liberating! With honesty and
humor, Regnier shows how forgiveness transformed her own life and
how it can be practiced in the family and in all our relationships."

DR. MARY HEALY
Scripture professor at Sacred Heart Major Seminary in Detroit,
author, and member of the Pontifical Biblical Commission

"This rich reflection on forgiveness will bring consolation, healing,
and peace to many. This book deserves a wide readership."

TERRENCE PRENDERGAST, SJ
Archbishop of Ottawa

"We are hearing much about mercy these days, especially with the popularity of the Divine Mercy devotion. But are we as eager to apply mercy to others as we are to have it applied to ourselves? We all have this powerful but difficult and costly ability. Priests, who hear confessions and offer counseling, can tell you that blocks to grace and progress in our spiritual life are often due to a lack of forgiveness, holding on to grudges, and withholding good will from those who have hurt us. How do we move on, let go, and release ourselves and others from unforgiveness's morbid grip? And how do we forgive ourselves, even when we know God has forgiven us? Angèle's book gives us a much-needed road map."

SR. HELENA BURNS, FSP
speaker and author of *He Speaks to You*

"*Forgiveness Is Key* is a heartfelt, honest, and humble invitation into the journey of forgiveness. It spoke deeply to my heart, and I know that anyone looking for deeper peace and freedom in his or her life will find great help and inspiration in this book."

SR. MIRIAM JAMES HEIDLAND, SOLT
speaker and author of *Loved as I Am*

FORGIVENESS IS KEY

A Personal Journey and Practical Guide for
Experiencing Mercy and Freedom

Angèle Regnier

Published by Ministry23, LLC
2401 Harnish Drive, Ste. 100
Algonquin, Illinois 60102
ministry23.com

Scripture quotations are from the *New Revised Standard Version Bible: Catholic Edition,* copyright © 1989, 1993 National Council of the Churches of Christ in the United States of America. Used by permission. All rights reserved.

Quotes marked *CCC* are taken from the English translation of the *Catechism of the Catholic Church for the United States of America,* 2nd ed. Copyright 1997 by United States Catholic Conference—Libreria Editrice Vaticana.

Cover design: Chris Pecora

NIHIL OBSTAT:
     Colin Kerr, PhD
     Censor deputatus
     December 31, 2015

IMPRIMATUR:
     Most Reverend Terrence Prendergast, SJ
     Archbishop of Ottawa
     January 4, 2016

ISBN 978-0-9965812-1-9

Printed in the United States of America

5 4 3 2 1

— ∾ **Contents** ∾ —

— ∽ **Introduction** ∾ —

"You will know the truth, and the truth will make you free."
—*John 8:32*

IN MARCH 1999 I sat in a pew, captivated by the preacher at our parish's Lenten Mission. Fr. Al Lauer, the founder of Presentation Ministries, said the most astonishing thing:

> *When I was first ordained a priest, I believed that over 50 percent of all problems were due to unforgiveness. After ten years in ministry, I revised my estimate and maintained 75 to 80 percent of all health, marital, family, and financial problems came from unforgiveness. Now, after more than twenty years in ministry, I have concluded that over 90 percent of all problems are rooted in unforgiveness.*

I couldn't believe my ears. Ninety percent! *Ninety percent?*

Maybe I could believe it…. My life's problems had been practically dripping all over the floor with unforgiveness for years. I was pretty sure Fr. Lauer had me pegged from his vantage point at the ambo. "That lady over there? Oh yeah, she's a 90-percenter for sure!"

For most of my life I didn't even know I was a 90-percenter. I was completely blind to it. In fact I would have classified myself as a zero-percenter if I had to scale it. I always prided myself on being a good forgiver as a kid—well, at least compared to all the other middle school girls.

That might sound like a ridiculous thing to be proud of, but if you've ever been around middle school girls, I think you know how that plays out. Any and every comment or action is subject to emotional overreaction and resentment (such as making the colossal mistake of wearing the same shirt as another girl, resulting in being ostracized for two weeks). For whatever reason, I never got worked up like those kinds of girls. I got over things very fast; I was quick to move on—like I said, I was a good forgiver. Once I even went up to a bully, who had humiliated me in front of the entire class, and told her I forgave her. What's more, I did it with her bully cohort watching on. Pretty impressive, right? Indeed.

I kept on impressing myself that way for almost three decades. And then I became bored with how nice I was, how good—and I did something kind of crazy. I prayed a dangerous prayer, even though I didn't realize it at the time: I asked God to show me my sin.

You see, Lent was approaching, and I wanted to have a different experience than I normally did. Every year on Good Friday, I wanted to experience personal sorrow for what Jesus did for me on the cross, but I could never feel it. I wanted an emotional reaction. I wanted to know that *I* had done this to Jesus; *my* sins had nailed him to the cross. I wanted to feel remorse. I really tried to muster up those feelings. The problem was that I didn't feel like a bad person for whom Jesus had to die, because…I wasn't a bad person. I was a very good person. My sins weren't nails coming at Jesus. They were more like marshmallows.

I was quite jealous of people who had dramatic stories of conversion. I was in awe of people who had been criminals or drug addicts before God intervened in their lives.

My story was not dramatic in the least; in fact, I considered it flat-out boring. I was raised in a Christian family and went to church all my life. I have always believed in God and in Jesus. I never chose to rebel from the faith and the way of life modeled for me by my family. I suppose I should be very grateful that God and his commandments were never hidden from me.

So as Lent 1996 approached, I prayed that God would show me the depth of my sin so I could truly appreciate the cross.

That Lent and Holy Week came and went, and by Easter Sunday I was eating chocolate bunnies with no greater understanding than I had before.

However, in the two or three years that followed, my spiritual journey took me to deep and dark places. The Holy Spirit unveiled incidents and relationships in my past that had caused me pain. The pain of these situations and people had locked me into resentment, fear, anger, lack of forgiveness, hatred, and other forms of rebellion in my life. I had never realized before how ugly and invasive the rot was. For the first time I saw that I had very serious sin in my life, and I understood that I needed God's mercy and grace to face it, be healed of it, and repent of it.

Fr. Al called it! Ninety percent is not a stretch.

A Light Shines in the Darkness

My husband and I are the founders of Catholic Christian Outreach, a university student movement dedicated to evangelization. We challenge students to live in the fullness of the Catholic Church with an emphasis on becoming leaders for the renewal of the world. From September to April CCO is on campus evangelizing and discipling, but from May to August we have the freedom to concentrate on other projects. During the summer of 1997, CCO invested significantly in exposing our full-time missionary staff to teaching and training on inner healing.

Inner healing ministry involves understanding the painful issues from one's past that influence how one responds in the present and how prayer can heal those wounds. I was pretty curious to find out what more I might learn about myself. I figured this should be interesting—a bit like taking a Myers-Briggs test.

Through the teachings I was given a new set of glasses to look at my life. What became all too evident was that I wasn't as good of a "forgiver" as I thought. My behaviour patterns, with their motivations and weaknesses, were revealed and exposed. Sure, I might have readily forgiven my classmates, but the hard truth was that I was locked in unforgiveness. I was stunned to discover the real state of my inner life.

It can be compared to doing a deep cleaning at home. You think your room is pretty clean. But when you start moving the bed or dressers away from the walls, you find all kinds of fuzz, dust, and nasty things. (Sometimes you find precious lost items and loose change, too! That can happen in the spiritual experience as well; God reveals good things, not just the mess.)

That summer the first thing the light exposed was that I had some huge hidden problems, especially with anger. And these had been kicking around for a long time.

Although I was an achiever at school, at home I acted differently. I was the classic bitter teenager. I often fought with my mom; I resented my brothers. In truest form I would create a scene about something I'm sure didn't really matter and then stomp off and sulk in my room. While this is pretty typical behaviour, for me it was also pretty loaded. There were two glaring sources of that anger: my mom and my "biological father," whom I feared and barely knew.

Origins

My parents divorced when I was three years old. Mom was only twenty-four when their marriage ended. You can imagine the kind of pain she must have been going through. Keep in mind that this was during the mid-1960s, and she was living in a small prairie community, having come from a traditional Catholic farming family. Divorce was rare and the source of social and religious shame.

It's interesting how kids pick up on things. I remember being cognisant that I was the only kid in the whole school—or the entire town, for that matter—that was from a broken home. I was only four, but I remember feeling ashamed and angry that I was not from a normal family. I acted out my confusion and pain about this rocky start to life by directing my anger toward my mother. I was an angry little girl.

But I was much more than angry at my father—I was terrified of him. I was afraid and repulsed by the thought of him. How could I have been so afraid of him at such a young age?

Again, kids pick up on things. Who knows what I had witnessed or absorbed in those tender years, but I can imagine that I picked up on my mom's anxiety and anguish as her marriage fell apart. This fact was underlined when Mom finally divulged to me as an adult that my father had threatened to abduct me in those early years. She shared how fearful she had been to let me out of her sight. Of course, she never told me any of this at the time, but knowing it now, I can see that I definitely picked up on her emotional state.

I wish I could take you into my reality and emotions as a little girl so you could understand how incredibly afraid I was. In my mind my father was very evil, and he was mean; he was someone I was very ashamed of.

I remember being afraid to leave my bed at night because of him. I was convinced he was waiting for me under my bed. I imagined him to be like the "boogey man" hiding under there, just waiting to catch me. Now this perception makes perfect sense in light of my mom's fear of my imminent abduction.

My anxiety every night was trying to figure out how to get in or out of bed. I was convinced that as soon I stepped out of bed, my father would snatch my legs and pull me under. I would jump as far as I could out of my bed when I left it and dive into it from as far a point as I could so he wouldn't catch me. This is a preschooler's understanding of who her father is?

When I got older my mom encouraged me to write letters to my dad, thanking him for the expensive gifts he sent for my birthday and Christmas. I hated her for asking me to do that. I felt responsible for maintaining a relationship with a man who was my mom's ex-husband more than he was my father. I never asked to have him as my father! I never chose him—she had. Why should I, a kid at that, carry the burden of her choices? I wanted nothing to do with this man. To make matters worse I looked a great deal like him. Every time I looked in the mirror, I was reminded of him, as if he had another place to haunt me.

All my life I hated this creepy mystery man who apparently was my father. I was angry at my mom for the whole messy situation— and I was undeniably mad at God, too. After all, wasn't all this ultimately his fault anyway? Why me? Why?

A Word of Caution

I have some concerns about writing a book with these themes. One concern is that this part of my life is very personal, and it takes a certain amount of emotional energy to recall it and unpack it.

But the biggest concern I have is that what I am sharing might be misunderstood—that you might think I'm blaming my parents.

Let me be perfectly clear: I have absolutely no desire to blame my parents by sharing my story. The inner healing course I took emphasized that digging up issues from the past, which for the most part involves one's parents, is not about blaming parents. It's about identifying, knowing, forgiving, and moving forward. My parents did the best they could in their particular circumstances. I can accept and appreciate that. Moreover, my intention is to focus attention on my own mistakes and bad attitudes, not theirs. I hope that comes through.

Another concern in sharing this story is that you might get overwhelmed with guilt about your own relationships. I wouldn't want you to hear my story and start thinking to yourself, *Oh man, what have I done to scar my kids or the people in my life? What if my kids get up in front of a microphone and tell everyone how I messed up their lives!*

Please avoid the temptation to become overwhelmed by any of this. I want this book to be a source of hope, not discouragement.

I am also concerned that by reading this book you might receive some of the practical tips I share in the wrong way—in a "self-help," fluffy kind of way. Although you are going to have to roll up your sleeves and play an active role to help yourself grow in forgiveness, you don't have to do this alone. This is where God wants to enter the scene. The Father will speak the truth of your real identity and belonging in him. The Holy Spirit will give you the courage and comfort to face and overcome painful situations. And Jesus, the source of all forgiveness and mercy, has made it possible for you to live in the freedom of forgiveness.

Questions for Personal Reflection

1. *What painful situations immediately come to mind as I read this chapter?*

2. *Who in my life comes to mind as someone I have a very hard time forgiving?*

3. *What aspects of my childhood are still sources of pain for me today? What are my earliest memories related to these painful issues?*

4. *Am I willing to reflect deeply on my life and give God permission to do whatever he needs to do in my heart while reading this book? If not, am I at least willing to be willing to give him permission to show me the healing I need?*

—◌ ONE ◌—
Why Forgive?

"Whenever you stand praying, forgive, if you have anything against anyone; so that your Father in heaven may also forgive you your trespasses."
—Mark 11:25

THE CITIZENS OF my city will never forget the incredible witness of the family of Ardeth Wood, a stunning twenty-seven-year-old graduate student who was brutally attacked and murdered along a Ottawa cycling path in 2003. Her family, a deeply faithful Catholic family, told *CBC News* that they forgave the assailant. They amazed an entire city shaken by Ardeth's tragic loss.

Why do people like the Woods forgive when the world says to hate and get even? I suspect they would tell you the same thing I am going to tell you now. It's a spiritual law nestled in the comforting words of the Lord's Prayer. I invite you not to skim over this famous prayer. Remember that familiarity breeds contempt. Take a moment, right now, to pray to the Father—slowly. And as you're praying, ask him to reveal to you the spiritual law embedded within. Let us pray:

> *Our Father, who art in heaven,*
> *hallowed be thy name;*
> *thy kingdom come;*
> *thy will be done,*
> *on earth as it is in heaven.*
> *Give us this day our daily bread.*
> *And forgive us our trespasses,*

as we forgive those who trespass against us.
And lead us not into temptation;
but deliver us from evil. Amen.

Did you identify the spiritual law? "Forgive us our trespasses, as we forgive those who trespass against us."

This is precisely what the Wood family did. They took Jesus at his word; they believed that he actually meant what he said—that he actually expects us to forgive others. To emphasise this expectation, Jesus actually makes our own forgiveness dependent upon it!

This is really a big deal. How often we have repeated those words by rote and not grasped how radically challenging they are! It's almost too much to wrap one's head around.

Three Convicting Truths

Praying the Lord's Prayer carefully marked the discovery of three convicting truths which rocked my entire world that summer of 1997.

1. Forgiveness Matters.

What I heard loud and clear in this simple and familiar phrase from the Our Father was that my own salvation was dependent on my forgiving others. God would forgive me only if I forgave others. But seriously, is Jesus really saying this?

It would be convenient if we could dismiss these words of Christ as being a one-off, isolated statement, but it isn't. As if he read our minds, anticipating we would say something like that, Jesus re-emphasises the point immediately after teaching us the Our Father. These are the two following verses:

> *"For if you forgive others their trespasses, your heavenly Father will also forgive you; but if you do not forgive others, neither will your Father forgive your trespasses." (Matthew 6:14–15)*

Notice the language is stronger this time. There's an "if" in there! *If:* It's a little word that packs a heck of a punch: "If you do not forgive others, neither will your Father forgive your trespasses." Jesus is trying to get our attention. Forgiveness matters! A lot! It makes sense to me now, but it didn't make sense to me then. Although I knew I forgave little things easily and quickly, I was now aware of the fact that I had not forgiven those who caused me big areas of pain. Had I tried to forgive them? Maybe I had. But I honestly don't know when or how or to what extent I had endeavoured to forgive. Even if I had attempted to forgive, the fact that I can't remember doing it isn't really a good sign.

What held me back from forgiving my parents thirty years ago was more than needing clarity and conviction about God's expectation to forgive. It was the fact that I felt justified in my bitterness. Although I wouldn't have been able to verbalize it at the time, the attitude of my heart was, "I was a victim of unfortunate circumstances. I have the right to be angry. No one would expect me to let go of bitterness in my situation."

If I had verbalized those words back then, as obviously wrong as I know they are now, I would have thought they made perfect sense. In my mind it was reasonable and logical that I should be exempt from having to forgive in light of the pain inflicted on me.

Although I didn't intentionally reject Scriptures passages like this classic one, I just glossed over them.

Then Peter came up and said to him, "Lord, how often shall my brother sin against me, and I forgive him? As many as seven times?" Jesus said to him, "I do not say to you seven times, but seventy times seven.

"Therefore the kingdom of heaven may be compared to a king who wished to settle accounts with his servants. When he began the reckoning, one was brought to him who owed him ten thousand talents; and as he could not pay, his lord ordered him to be sold, with his wife and children and all that he had, and payment to be made. So the servant fell on his knees, imploring him, 'Lord, have patience with me, and I will pay you everything.' And out of pity for him the lord of that servant released him and forgave him the

debt. But that same servant, as he went out, came upon one of his fellow servants who owed him a hundred denarii; and seizing him by the throat he said, 'Pay what you owe.' So his fellow servant fell down and besought him, 'Have patience with me, and I will pay you.' He refused and went and put him in prison till he should pay the debt. When his fellow servants saw what had taken place, they were greatly distressed, and they went and reported to their lord all that had taken place. Then his lord summoned him and said to him, 'You wicked servant! I forgave you all that debt because you besought me; and should not you have had mercy on your fellow servant, as I had mercy on you?' And in anger his lord delivered him to the jailers, till he should pay all his debt. So also my heavenly Father will do to every one of you, if you do not forgive your brother from your heart." (Matthew 18:21–35)

I somehow figured verses like this didn't apply to me. I rationalized that this Scripture passage must be referring to forgiving someone who was guilty of a lesser offense. I forgave those who had minor offenses against me readily and willingly. It just didn't compute that I had to apply this to any of the big offenses.

I rationalised that God wouldn't punish me for not forgiving: *I'm a good person. He loves me, after all.* Whenever I heard the "seventy times seven" verse, I remember thinking, *If someone is going to repeat sinning against me 490 times, that's simply unacceptable. Jesus can't really expect me to keep forgiving that kind of a repeat offender. That would just be ridiculous! I think it's totally justified not to forgive that kind of a person. I don't believe this is what Jesus would be saying. How could we say something like this? It doesn't make sense.*

I really believed this! I had convinced myself—or maybe it was the enemy who had convinced me—to twist the Scriptures to say something Jesus wasn't saying.

I also managed to dodge Scripture passages where Jesus asked us to forgive those who have gravely offended us and do not deserve our mercy:

"But I say to you that listen, Love your enemies, do good to those who hate you, bless those who curse you, pray for those who abuse you. If anyone strikes you on the cheek, offer the other also; and from anyone who takes away your coat do not withhold even your shirt. Give to everyone who begs from you; and if anyone takes away your goods, do not ask for them again. Do to others as you would have them do to you.

"If you love those who love you, what credit is that to you? For even sinners love those who love them. If you do good to those who do good to you, what credit is that to you? For even sinners do the same. If you lend to those from whom you hope to receive, what credit is that to you? Even sinners lend to sinners, to receive as much again. But love your enemies, do good, and lend, expecting nothing in return. Your reward will be great, and you will be children of the Most High; for he is kind to the ungrateful and the wicked. Be merciful, just as your Father is merciful.

"Do not judge, and you will not be judged; do not condemn, and you will not be condemned. Forgive, and you will be forgiven; give, and it will be given to you. A good measure, pressed down, shaken together, running over, will be put into your lap; for the measure you give will be the measure you get back." (Luke 6:27–38)

Did you notice how Jesus opens that whole discourse by saying, "I say to you that listen..." No wonder I was never convicted by those kinds of Scripture passages—I really wasn't listening.

However, I hope you *are* listening. "Let those who have ears hear!"

Once I started listening and really grasped this convicting truth, I was shocked that I hadn't realized what Jesus was really saying! He was saying that forgiveness is required and necessary. If we want to be forgiven, we must forgive. We can't afford to gloss over this truth. Our soul depends on it. It's that serious. He is asking us—no, it's more than that—he is *requiring* us to do so in kind. Forgiveness matters. Forgiveness is key.

2. I Am Part of the Problem.

The second big convicting truth I encountered that summer was that I, too, was part of the problem.

How can that be? Wasn't I just a little kid, a victim in this whole messy situation?

I might have been a victim, but I also had done things as a result of the circumstances of my life that I needed to acknowledge before God. This might be hard to grasp, but bear with me as I explain.

The Lord opened my eyes to see that there were serious things I needed to repent of, that I was completely clueless about: namely refusing to forgive. I willingly and deliberately held on to resentment, judgment, bitterness, and unforgiveness. And as we have seen in the Scripture passages quoted, this is an extremely serious sin. My salvation was dependent on my response to this teaching, but I had denied its truth and relevance to my life.

I was also convicted of another serious sin—that of dishonouring my parents. I had conveniently dismissed this Scripture as well. Everyone disrespects our parents, anyway, right? No need to get too worked up about this one! There I was again, fashioning the truth to suit my own preferences. This is one of the Ten Commandments, after all! Dishonouring one's parents is a serious issue in God's eyes. It actually matters to him.

It sobered me to recognize how extensively I had dishonoured my mom. I am sorry to admit that I was very mean to her. The majority of my interactions with her were laced with anger and attitude. I punished her out of bitterness in almost every interaction. I purposefully withheld love from her. It's understandable that a child or teenager would act out it this way due to pain, but even children and teens can learn to forgive (and often are better models of this than adults).

My being "part of the problem" was that I continued to act in this way into my adult life. I realized for the first time that my sins—in particular, those against my mother—were worse than any of her failures toward me. Her failures were mistakes or bad decisions; mine were more serious. I was justifying unforgiveness, resentment, and dishonouring my parents, all grave matters of sin. And what's more, I should have known better, especially as a mature Christian leader.

Once I saw these truths coming into focus, I was immediately convicted. "Lord, I don't want to be in rebellion to your will like this! I've harboured so much bitterness and justified my anger. How could I have been so foolish?"

Not only is honouring one's parents important enough to God to be one of the Ten Commandments, it's also the only commandment with a promise. Check it out: "Honor your father and your mother, so that your days may be long in the land that the LORD your God is giving you" (Exodus 20:12).

There are other Scripture verses which speak not only of the importance of honouring one's parents, but the ramifications of dishonouring them on future generations (see Matthew 15:4; Proverbs 30:17; Leviticus 20:9). I desired God's blessing on my future, but I *really* desired it for my children's future, and that meant I needed to honour my parents.

The Lord revealed another serious, sinful habit that kept me steeped in bitterness and unforgiveness: judging people.

> *"Do not judge, so that you may not be judged. For with the judgment you make you will be judged, and the measure you give will be the measure you get. Why do you see the speck in your neighbor's eye, but do not notice the log in your own eye? Or how can you say to your neighbor, 'Let me take the speck out of your eye,' while the log is in your own eye? You hypocrite, first take the log out of your own eye, and then you will see clearly to take the speck out of your neighbor's eye." (Matthew 7:1–7)*

I had to face the fact that I am quite proficient in judging people. Being judgmental is the product of my angry heart and low self-esteem; cutting others down is a way to make myself feel better. Judging others is how I operate. Kind of like the T-shirts that were popular with psychology grad students when I went to university: "Yes, I'm in Psychology. Yes, I'm analyzing you, and frankly I'm concerned."

I judged how people talked, what they wore, how they did their hair, how they stood, what they ate, and how they ate. I judged the way they thought. I judged them for being boring, weird, mean, or dumb. I judged them for hating me. I judged them for judging me, and I was infuriated at the thought!

In the parallel passage in Luke's Gospel, Jesus says, "Do not judge, and you will not be judged; do not condemn, and you will not be condemned. Forgive, and you will be forgiven" (Luke 6:37). Just look at all the times "you" is used in that verse! I remember thinking, *If Jesus is really serious here—and I have no good reason to think he's not being serious—and he is warning me that he will judge, condemn, and forgive me as harshly as I have judged, condemned, and forgiven others (especially my parents), then I'm in big trouble!*

There were so many lightbulbs going off in the recesses of my soul! The light of Christ was exposing sinful attitudes left, right, and centre. I was seeing the rot that had lain dark, hidden, and unrecognizable for so long. I was not only getting a sense of how extensive it was, but how complicit I was in it.

God was not only challenging me to full-out forgiveness, he was also asking me to repent and own up for my side of the story. I had no excuse for my behaviour, other than the fact that I was blinded with resentment and had ignored the truth in the Scriptures. Frankly I'm surprised that God put up with me—I was waltzing around thinking I was a perfectly devout Christian, but the whole while I was stinking to high heaven with the rot of all kinds of nasty sin and judgements.

3. Unforgiveness Is a Prison.

Someone once said, "Resentment is like taking poison and expecting the other person to die." Withholding forgiveness was my way of inflicting revenge and punishing my parents. I was locking them out of my life. What I didn't realize was that they were locked out simply by virtue of the fact that I was the one locked in.

Fr. Al Lauer, in his brochure, *The Book on Forgiveness*, quotes St. John Paul II as saying, "Forgiveness is the restoration of freedom to oneself. It is the key held in our own hand to our prison cell."[1]

That's it! I was a prisoner to my own unforgiveness. Unforgiveness

---

1 Fr. Al Lauer, *The Book of Forgiveness*, Presentation Ministries, http://www.presentationministries.com/brochures/BookOnForgiveness.asp.

had locked me into a deep unhappiness. I was imprisoned in anger, fear, and bitterness. The person punished the most in all of this was me—not my mom, and certainly not my biological father (who, due to the most minimal communications, would have been unaware of my emotional outbursts and bitterness). No, the biggest casualty in it all was me.

I presumed that the only beneficiary of forgiveness was the one being forgiven. I saw forgiveness as an act of generosity, letting the offender off of the hook so he or she could be free to live their life. That is true, but forgiveness is much more than that. It's also what Fr. Al Lauer said: "Forgiveness is the restoration of freedom to oneself."[2]

This brings to mind the character of Inspector Javert from the musical *Les Misérables*. In order to somehow compensate for the disreputable life of his parents, Javert is obsessed with justice. This is an admirable virtue, but without mercy it risks missing balance and goodness in its execution. At Mass we say, "It is right and just"; Javert only caught the latter. Justice requires goodness or rightness to keep it balanced.

Throughout the story Inspector Javert is obsessed with unearthing the true identity of M. le Maire—the man he is convinced is really the criminal he knew as Jean Valjean.

Jean Valjean, upon his parole, had a conversion and was living a "new life"—an upright life under a false identity, bringing work and dignity to the villagers of Montreuil-sur-mer, where he was mayor.

Jean Valjean eventually is forced to reveal his true identity to protect the life of a man mistaken for himself. The punishment for breaking the rules of his parole is life imprisonment. Jean does not want this for himself, but neither can he let another be wrongfully jailed in his place. When Javert hears of Jean Valjean's confession, he seeks to bring him to full justice and punishment. Jean Valjean flees and goes into hiding, where for many years he lives a life of virtue protected by cloistered walls.

Javert never wavers in his search for Jean Valjean, and he succeeds in tracking him down almost a decade later. At one point Jean Valjean has the upper hand and could end Javert's life, but instead he gives him the chance to escape. He has no desire to kill the inspector;

2 Ibid.

he just wants him to leave him alone so he can live a peaceful, honourable life. Javert, fixated on justice, returns once again to hunt for Jean Valjean, convinced that he is a criminal incapable of reform who must be punished.

As the story draws to a close, we see the predicament Javert's worldview has caused him. In his mind justice is incompatible with mercy. He sees no way to resolve the two. He cannot simply let Jean Valjean go free; he must subject him to the demands of justice. He notices Jean Valjean's integrity and goodness, but it doesn't compute. Valjean is a criminal; that is his lot in life and he must be punished. Unable to reconcile mercy with justice, Javert takes his own life to end the gnawing confusion of his internal logic.

Javert was locked into judgement about who Jean Valjean was and what he had done. In his judgement, there could be no mercy and no hope of redemption. The judgement he imposed was the judgement he received. "For with the judgement you make you will be judged." Mercy was not an option, even for himself. He would not be satisfied until Jean Valjean was in prison, but in truth it was he who was living a life that was punished and tormented.

I saw myself in Javert. You might not have known it by looking at me. (I think we're all pretty good at making ourselves pleasant and presentable to others.) But I was a prisoner and slave to my anger and bitterness. The teachings we were getting in our inner healing course were undeniably exposing my state of affairs. The more I saw, the more I longed for freedom. I wanted it so badly I could taste it. I was sick of the baggage, sick of the prison, and ready to do whatever it took to get out. This place of being sick and tired of your rot is a great grace. It is fertile ground that readies the heart for healing, forgiveness, and restoration.

The Scriptures talk about God loosening the chains of bondage as an allegory to our slavery to sin: "On that day, says the LORD of hosts, I will break the yoke from off his neck, and I will burst his bonds" (Jeremiah 30:8). Someone explained to me that God loosens the chains, but we have to step out of them. We must choose to live in the freedom of children of God. "You will know the truth, and the truth will make you free" (John 8:32).

Up until the summer of 1997, I thought I was going along in life quite nicely, thank you very much. I was a full-time lay missionary, a mother of three, and a devoted wife. Remember how I considered myself to be an exceptionally good person and how I prayed that I could have a more poignant connection with Good Friday? That prayer had taken place just over a year earlier, and now God was doing some serious renovation work on my heart.

If God in his great love and mercy—through the passion, death, and resurrection of Christ—loved me and rescued me and forgave me for all my failures, weaknesses, and sins, how could I withhold forgiveness from another? The reality was that I had done serious things, I'm a repeat offender, I don't deserve forgiveness or eternal life, but God was offering it to me out of his gratuitous love. It was an invitation to receive and to give mercy.

Questions for Personal Reflection

1. *When I hear the words "Forgive us our trespasses, as we forgive those who trespass against us," what situations or people come to mind? What are those hurts and who are those individuals in my life that God is asking me to release and forgive?*

2. *How have I tried to forgive those who have wronged me? If I haven't tried to forgive them, why not? How might I have rationalized that I do not need to forgive them?*

3. *How is unforgiveness working for me? How effective am I at punishing the people I resent? What effect does my unforgiveness have on my life, my joy, my peace, my freedom?*

4. *Am I ready and willing to do something about my bitterness and resentment? Am I sick and tired of it?*

─ ∞ TWO ∞ ─

Afraid to Forgive

"Do you not realize that God's kindness is meant to lead you to repentance?"
—*Romans 2:4b*

I WAS READY for whatever God wanted me to do to move forward on this forgiveness stuff. I was committed to responding to those three convicting truths:

1. *God requires us to forgive in order to be forgiven.*
2. *I am part of the problem.*
3. *I am a prisoner to my unforgiveness.*

Catching these truths and seeing them as true in my life was obviously the first step. The next steps required action. How appropriate that *forgive* is a verb! Merriam-Webster defines it in this way: "to stop feeling anger toward (someone who has done something wrong); to stop blaming (someone); to stop feeling anger about (something); to forgive someone for (something wrong); or to stop requiring payment of (money that is owed)."[3]

This is a very helpful definition. I especially like the last definition, "to stop requiring payment of money that is owed." From a Christian perspective, this reminds us of how Jesus's death on the cross was the atonement that "paid" or expiated our sin. He is the Lamb of God who takes away the sin of the world. As St. Paul wrote:

---

3 http://www.merriam-webster.com/dictionary/forgive.

And when you were dead in trespasses and the uncircumcision of your flesh, God made you alive together with him, when he forgave us all our trespasses, erasing the record that stood against us with its legal demands. He set this aside, nailing it to the cross. (Colossians 2:14)

The *Catechism of the Catholic Church* explains how Jesus makes reparation for us in the words of Consecration at Mass:

Jesus gave the supreme expression...of his voluntary offering to the Father for the salvation of men: "This is my body which is given for you.... This is my blood of the covenant, which is poured out for many for the forgiveness of sins." (CCC, 610)

In him, through his flesh and blood sacrificed as a sin offering, our forgiveness was accomplished once and for all.

The verb *forgive* is an action, but in most of the definitions above, you'll notice the action is "to stop." That's an interesting action, I guess. To *stop* means "to not do something that you have been doing before." It's essentially a choice, an act of the will.

When we forgive we choose to let go of resentment we are harbouring for the sins committed against us. We choose to renounce the right to exact vengeance on the one who has hurt us. We release that person to be judged by God, not by us. We entrust the situation, and our justice, to God's hands.

Lessons from *Cinderella*

In Disney's 2015 *Cinderella* movie, the concept of forgiveness is part of two specific scenes—one at the beginning and one at the end. Early in the movie, the delightful world of Ella's family is in jeopardy with the imminent death of her mother. Her parting words to her daughter were, "Ella, I must go very soon, my love. Please forgive me."[4]

---

4 *Cinderella*, DVD, directed by Kenneth Branagh (Burbank, Calif.: Walt Disney Studios, 2015).

Forgive? That's a curious thing for a dying mother to say to her child! Ella has a beautiful relationship with her mother—what could possibly need to be forgiven?

Ella's mother wants to know that she is leaving with their relationship in right order; she wants the assurance that Ella has released her and allowed her to go. She knows it is hard for a child not to resent her mother's death. She needs to know that Cinderella will not be trapped in bitterness and pain. She wants Cinderella to live in freedom. She is asking Ella to let her go. She needs to hear the words which will bring them both peace: "Of course I forgive you."

At the close of the film, we see Ella facing the decision to embrace the same disposition of forgiveness and releasing. Even though she is locked in the attic by her wicked stepmother, her spirit is not a prisoner to her surroundings. Her singing voice rises above her circumstances and carries out the window to the ears of the king's men, who release her from her attic prison. As she is about to leave with the prince, she stops and turns toward her stepmother and says three simple words: "I forgive you." She says them with composure, sincerity, and lightness. And although she says "I forgive you" so delicately, everyone in the scene knows that these three little words are powerful, loaded with the weight and duration of the injustices she suffered at her stepmother's hands.

Forgiveness in Ella's context means, "I release you. I will stop feeling anger toward you. I will stop blaming you. I will stop feeling anger about what you did to my life and my family home. I will not demand that you pay me back for what you did to me. I am letting it go."

Ella knows that even though she has been released from her attic prison, unforgiveness would keep her a prisoner in her heart. She chooses to release her enemy and herself through the power of forgiveness. And she does so with poise, integrity, and not even a hint of vengeance.

Letting go, releasing, relinquishing, dropping, stopping, freeing—these synonyms are attitudes as well as actions. They begin in the deepest place of our hearts, as a decision to change our attitude from pain or revenge to release. That paradigm shift in our attitude governs how we then act. The attitude shift prompts us to stop how we would normally respond and to go further, to act with mercy.

Mercy is showing kindness to someone who doesn't deserve it, someone you have the right to punish. A proper Christian understanding of forgiveness is more than just holding back or stopping punishment, hatred, or vengeance. It's also a choice for mercy—choosing to love our enemies.

The Christian call to love doesn't require cuddling or holding hands with your enemies. The love we are talking about here is a sincere desire that your enemies are blessed. It is wanting good for them. Let me tell you, if you can get to a place in your wounded relationships where you have the freedom to love the people who have harmed you by saying, "I sincerely wish them well, and I will be happy for them to be blessed in life," you have come a long way, my friend, and I assure you that you are living out of love and mercy.

This is God's grace. You could only act this way, and have this change of heart, by and through God's help. It is nothing short of a divine intervention in your life, which transforms you interiorly and gives you the freedom to show mercy.

Natural questions that may be going through your mind at this point include concerns for justice and protection of the one who has been victimized. Does forgiveness mean allowing abuse to continue? No! Forgiveness never means that hurtful actions are okay. Forgiveness is ultimately an act of obedience to the command to forgive, and obeying the Lord doesn't end there. We continue to obey the Lord by following his prompting regarding how to remove ourselves from the abusive situation.

Forgiveness is not saying it's okay for people to keep hurting us. But forgiveness does ask us to keep forgiving even as they continue to hurt us—seventy times seven times.

"God Will Give Me Justice"

Forgiveness is saying, "I choose to release you into God's hands, and I give up any rights I think I have to exact justice, because I know that God will give me justice."

"God will give me justice" are the words of the graffiti etched in the prison cell of Edmond Dantès, the character played by Jim Caviezel in the movie adaptation of *The Count of Monte Cristo*. Dantès, a virtuous, hardworking young man, is framed by his best friend and sentenced to solitary confinement for life at the Chateau d'If Prison. While in his cell, he scratches over and over again the words "God will give me justice." I suspect that initially Edmond was scratching those words from a place of entrusting the situation to God. But as the years of his imprisonment pass, it is clear that the phrase is not a prayer of entrustment; it has become a demand—a shaking of his fist toward God: "You owe me justice!"

I have to confess this movie is one of my all-time favourites because of the way it paints the themes of betrayal, vengeance, forgiveness, and God's justice and care. I wouldn't want my description of the movie to be a spoiler for your enjoyment of it, but I will say that God does give Dantès justice in time. By the end of the movie, he recognizes the freedom forgiveness gives that vengeance cannot. He is able to look back on everything that happened and see God's hand in it all, despite the choices others made that affected his life.

God is in everything, but God also doesn't control everything and everyone like a puppet show. He gave us all free will. The rub is that one person's free will and actions necessarily have ramifications on others. God isn't in heaven pulling the strings and making everyone behave properly. Maybe life would have been much tidier if God had created us as puppets or robots, but he didn't. He created us with the freedom to choose and the freedom to love. Freedom means people can choose poorly, too. God, being God, has his own creative ways of using the bad to bring about an even greater good. His goodness is not limited by the power we wield with the free will he gave us. The truth is that his goodness, mercy, and love triumph over everything and anything this world can throw at us—be it in this life or the next. We won't be left more vulnerable because we choose to release and forgive. God will give us justice in his time. We can count on it; we can actively wait for it.

I believe that I shall see the goodness of the LORD
in the land of the living.
Wait for the LORD;

31

be strong, and let your heart take courage;
wait for the LORD! (Psalm 27:13–14)

Sometimes in our prayerful listening and waiting for the Lord to direct us to a safer situation, we don't see an immediate solution. We can't start thinking that God is busy at the moment with other important cosmic matters until he can focus a little time on us. We have to believe he is Sovereign, Lord and Master, King of the Universe. We need to be confident that "he's got this."

The Lord is my rock, my fortress, and my deliverer, my God, my rock in whom I take refuge, my shield, and the horn of my salvation, my stronghold. (Psalm 18:2)

O my God, in you I trust; do not let me be put to shame; do not let my enemies exult over me. (Psalm 25:2)

The psalmist models how to trust in God's care despite one's circumstances. We can find a refuge and solace, even in the midst of chaos, in our innermost being where we commune with the Lord and know his love. We can know an interior freedom and peace that no one can steal from us despite our circumstances. The saints and martyrs witness to this.

St. Maximilian Kolbe, despite the appalling situation at Auschwitz, did not cease to encourage others and call them to prayer and faith. He was a steady rock because of the communion he had with God in the interior castle of his heart. From this place St. Maximilian Kolbe certainly received the grace to choose to forgive his captors, entrusting them and himself to God's hands.

Forgiveness is ultimately rooted in a deep confidence in God's sovereignty and goodness. If I know I'm cared for by God, I can release my pain and entrust those who caused it to his care.

The Trinity

As I have been trusting in God's care for me more and more, he has led me to understand his protection and love uniquely as it relates to each of the Persons of the Trinity. I know that I am only scratching the surface, but even this little bit of knowledge is mind-blowing. I am getting to know the unwavering and ever-present goodness of the Father. I am learning to lean on the Holy Spirit, who comes alongside me to support me and empower me in my struggles. And then there's Jesus. He is my rescuer and protector, who has proven his immense desire to love me and save me.

The Father: Goodness

Fundamentally each of us needs to know the Father's love for us. We long to know that we are wanted, that we matter, that we belong, that we are cherished, that we are safe and protected. It makes sense that we long to know these things, because they are true of our Heavenly Father. We instinctively seek out the characteristics of our true Father. It's almost as if we are sniffing him out and finding him the way baby animals somehow find the scent of their mother.

It is incredible that Almighty God has chosen to reveal himself to us through the imagery of fatherhood.

> For all who are led by the Spirit of God are children of God. For you did not receive a spirit of slavery to fall back into fear, but you have received a spirit of adoption. When we cry, "Abba! Father!" it is that very Spirit bearing witness with our spirit that we are children of God. (Romans 8:14–16)

Because my childhood experience was one of abandonment, my heart has a hard time understanding God the Father, let alone believing that he is caring, present, good, and protective of me. St. Thérèse of Lisieux is a saint who has helped me think about God as my Father. I want my heart and mind to perceive things the way she does with her childlike trust: "Expect all things from the good God just as a little child expects all things from its father; it is not to be troubled by anything."[5]

---

5 St. Thérèse of Lisieux, quoted in Paul Marie de la Croix, ODC, "St. Therese's Life in the Carmel of Lisieux and the Influence of Her 'Little Way,'" in Carmelite Spirituality (Washington, DC: ICS Publications, 1997), https://www.ewtn.com/therese/carmel.htm.

If I could really know and trust that the Father is good, what confidence I would have! I would have confidence to believe that he is taking care of me no matter what.

My husband, André, is a great dad. He has been a living example to our children of the Heavenly Father's goodness and protection. Our kids have grown up confidently in that care. An example of this confidence is illustrated with a story I call "The Day No One Came to Pick Up Janna." We have five kids, and our schedule, like most people's these days, can get chaotic. Janna was at the parish for her sacramental preparation class, which ended at 6:30 p.m. At 7:45 p.m. her catechists started to wonder where we were. Why wasn't anyone coming to pick up Janna?

Janna was oblivious to any anxiety as she waited. She was enjoying her time in the narthex— chatting with Father Yves, looking at the statue of St. Joseph, and checking out the colouring sheets in the kids' area. At some point one of the catechists approached her and said gently, hoping the concern she had would not alarm her, "Janna dear, do you know who is coming to pick you up from class?"

Janna raised her eyebrows as she tried to recall who might be coming to get her. "Umm, I don't know. Someone." She shrugged her shoulders, smiled, and skipped off to look at the photos on the Youth Ministry bulletin board.

Her catechists were amazed at this seven-year-old confidence. She wasn't frightened or fretful. She just knew she was loved and would be cared for by her family. Although all the members of the family contributed to her growing up in an environment of love and care, her special bond with her dad cannot be underestimated.

What if we had that kind of deeply rooted, childlike confidence in God the Father? What if we had that confidence despite the circumstances, despite the waiting? If we had that kind of relationship of love and security, handing over our right to anger and vengeance into the capable hands of our Dad would not be difficult to do. It would be the kind of experience in which we know a problem is going to be taken care of properly and we don't have to worry.

Sometimes people are icons, or pictures, of God for me. Their character and virtues model some aspect of how to grasp who God is.

I know these are imperfect people, but they help me paint the picture in my mind of some aspects of God's goodness. I encourage you to think of someone (or perhaps multiple "someones") who reminds you of some aspect of what God the Father might be like. If no one in your sphere of influence comes to mind, perhaps there is a character from film or literature that might frame an idea of what the Father is like.

I find this kind of exercise helpful because I have always perceived God the Father within the same framework as my experience of my biological father. "I apparently have a father; he's out there somewhere, I guess. I don't know him but I occasionally get gifts from him. Although he knows I'm his daughter, he definitely doesn't know me. I doubt that he really cares too much about me based on his lack of support and engagement. He's seems pretty mysterious and hidden, and I'm pretty sure he can't be trusted. In fact, I'm not sure if he is good at all. It's probably best that he keeps his distance, because he'd probably ruin my life anyway." That's a pretty accurate description of how I viewed God the Father. He was out there somewhere, but he wasn't there for me.

To heal this perception, God has put a handful of portraits of his fatherhood in my life—not the least of which is my "dad," my mom's second husband. He has been the only dad I've really known, since he came into our lives when I was four years old. He is a gentle, warm, fun-loving, generous, and tender man. He accepted me into his life as though I had always been his very own daughter.

Another icon for me of the Father is that of a distinguished, faithful man I met at a congress in Rome. Immediately upon meeting Dr. Luis, people are aware of his unique presence. He is eloquent, handsome, gracious, intelligent, with eyes which are kind but also somehow serious at the same time. I had the pleasure of visiting with him over several meals, and I was able to share with him our evangelistic faith study, *Discovery*, which had just been translated into Spanish. The next morning he came downstairs for breakfast and made a beeline for me, telling me he had read the whole book the night before in his room. He planned to use it with the Catholic students at the Latin American university where he was Dean of Medicine. And then the icon of the

Father was made known to me in a very personal way. He put his hands on my shoulders, kissed my forehead, and said, "Congratulations. Well done."

This was unmistakeably the kiss of the Father for me. I never knew if God knew what I was doing for him! I never knew he was proud of me. I wasn't sure I was even on his radar!

A year later at a follow-up gathering to that congress, I struck up a conversation on the bus with a participant who was from the same country as Dr. Luis. "Oh, do you know Dr. Luis?" I asked. "I met him here last year. He is such a wonderful man!"

"But of course I know him; everyone in my country knows him!"

"Oh, really? Is he a famous doctor or medical researcher? I know he's the Dean of the Faculty of Medicine at his university…"

The gentleman put his hand over his mouth to conceal his laughter. "Oh, that's not why we all know him. I guess you don't know. He used to be the prime minister of our country."

No wonder he came across so confidently and eloquently! No wonder he exuded authority and wisdom when he spoke. But he was more than the embodiment of classic leadership strengths; he was also kind, gentle, and good. This man, who had been an icon of the Father's love to me a year before, was now brought into sharper focus. The tender affection and affirmation I received came not only from a kind man, but from a man of authority. I could picture the Father in a particular way now, as a good man who engendered trust, exuded authority, and naturally elicited respect. A Father like this can be trusted to take care of me. A Father like this, who is a ruler of a country or kingdom, wields the authority to make things happen. A Father like this can and will take care of his daughter's needs.

Now I have a better picture of the Father. The icon I have is a man in a sharply tailored suit with distinguished grey hair, kind eyes, and a resolute brow, who looks at me and says, "Angèle, I am taking care of this." And you know what? I know he is.

"Look at the birds of the air; they neither sow nor reap nor gather into barns, and yet your heavenly Father feeds them. Are you not of more value than they?" (Matthew 6:26)

"If you then, who are evil, know how to give good gifts to your children, how much more will your Father in heaven give good things to those who ask him!" (Matthew 7:11)

This perception of the Father allows me to shift my paradigm when it comes to forgiving others. If forgiveness means letting go of my right to hate or retaliate due to the sins committed against me, I can release it into this Father's hands. I can picture a Father like this protecting me and making sure everything will be dealt with. I can follow his lead and his word. If he tells me I need to obey him by forgiving, choosing mercy, and leaving justice in his hands, how can I say no to that face? How can I not trust and be completely confident in his care, goodness, and protection? "Yes, I'm in very good hands. Yes, I will trust the kindness and authority in your eyes. I can let it go. I can pray with confidence 'Thy will be done on earth, as it is in heaven' because I believe in your love for me."

Holy Spirit: Defense Lawyer

Sometimes I feel bad for the Holy Spirit. He is so often ignored and misunderstood. He's the third Person of the Trinity, but we so often trivialize him down to the level of a white felt dove glued to a burlap banner in our parishes. Talk about poor PR!

Romans 5:5 is one of my favourite verses about the Holy Spirit: "God's love has been poured into our hearts through the Holy Spirit that has been given to us." The Holy Spirit is characterized primarily as the love between the Father and the Son. The Holy Spirit is also understood as the breath of God and the power of God—at once gentle inspiration and magnificent power.

As amazing as the Holy Spirit is, what has had the most enduring impact on me personally is how Jesus describes him in John 14:16. He refers to him as *Paraclete*, a Greek word translated as "Advocate." The reason I like this so much is that he is described as a defense lawyer. What a defense lawyer to have on your side!

One day at a retreat, I ended up lending a listening ear and some counsel to someone I had just met in a small-group sharing. In the course of his story, he shared how concerned he was because he was looking for work. He was less upset about the pressure of finding work than about how he ended up in this situation in the first place. He lost his previous job through the lies and betrayal of his supervisor. As he unpacked his story, his pain and anger became more and more unmasked. As he discussed all the possible avenues for revenge and retaliation, I asked him what he thought the Lord wanted him to do about the situation.

He seemed befuddled by this question and very uncomfortable about the idea of leaving justice in God's hands. He then asked me, "Do you think God expects me to forgive him?" in a tone that communicated, "There's no way God would ever expect me to forgive this!"

I knew this was a sensitive issue for him. So I took my time and then said ever so slowly and gently, "Yeah. Yeah, he does." He shook his head in disbelief.

I gently reminded him that Jesus asked the Father to forgive those who were crucifying him. I reminded him of the words of the Our Father. I could have kept going, but it wasn't necessary. He was a man of faith, and deep down he knew he needed to forgive.

It was at this point that I took a different approach and talked to him about the Holy Spirit as the Paraclete. I said, "What you really need for justice to occur is to take him to court, right? Can you imagine how confident and cared for you would feel if you had the means to hire the best defense lawyer in the country to plead your case? Better yet, what if you had at your disposal the best defense lawyer in the world? How assured would you feel that things would turn out in your favour—that justice would be served?"

"I would be more than confident. I would just know he would win the case for me."

"Exactly. And that is what the Holy Spirit is for you in this situation. Jesus describes the Holy Spirit as the Paraclete, or Advocate—which essentially means 'defense lawyer.' He comes alongside you and supports, comforts, counsels, and guides you on what to do. You have the best legal defense for justice in the universe on your side. He's not only the best lawyer available; he's also your closest friend. He deeply cares about you and your welfare. He loves you. The question is: Will you trust that this entire situation is in the hands of the Holy Spirit, the Advocate? Will you trust his guidance? Will you obey his lead and do what he asks you to do, as you would follow a great lawyer's advice for strategy in court? The first thing the Holy Spirit is asking you to do is obvious; he is indeed asking you to forgive. He's also asking you to trust that he will take care of your needs, that even though the situation has been unjust and terrible, he will bless you abundantly for your faithfulness and obedience to him."

I then shared this inspiring quotation by Fr. Jean D'Elbee:

> *He will bring good out of evil and even, as I have already told you, a greater good than if there had been no evil; and the trial will have been an immense good for us.*[6]

I wish I could tell you what came out of that conversation, but I never saw the man again. All I can say is that when we parted ways, he was facing a huge challenge to believe what God was saying in Scripture—that he needed to forgive his enemy, and that the Holy Spirit promised to be his Advocate. I hope that he had a good long consult with his Defense Lawyer and realized he could leave justice in his capable hands.

Jesus: My Rescuer

The perspective with which I approach Jesus in terms of forgiveness is that of a hero who goes to the ends of the earth and to the direst of circumstances to rescue me from danger and death. This is kind of a Hollywood way of describing the gospel message, but it works for me. Indiana Jones, Peter Parker, and Tony Stark have nothing on Jesus Christ.

Jesus laid down his life willingly, painfully, and with great humiliation so we could live. He had only to lift a finger and at his command legions of angels would have rushed to his defense. But he stayed his hand and allowed the consequences of the sin of each and every human being to be borne in his body. His courage and tenacity

---

6 Jean D'Elbee, *I Believe in Love: A Personal Retreat Based on the Teaching of St. Thérèse of Lisieux* (Manchester, NH: Sophia Press, 2001), 91.

to fight for us at all costs despite our rebellion and rejection is amazing. But his love for us cannot be held back; its reach is endless.

I love Jesus Culture's song from the album of the same title, *Unstoppable Love*. The way Christa Black Gifford and Kim Walker-Smith wrote these lyrics inspires me to trust Jesus. If this is the kind of love he has for me, how could I hold anything back from him, or fear what could come my way with him at my side?

Try to stop Your love, and
You would wage a war
Try to take the very thing,
You gave Your life for
You would come running, tear down every wall
All the while shouting,
"My love you're worth it all!"

God, You pursue me, with power and glory
Unstoppable love that never ends
You're unrelenting, with passion and mercy
Unstoppable love that never ends

No sin, no shame, no past, no pain
Can separate me from Your love
No height, no depth, no fear, no death
Can separate me from Your love.[7]

Notice that the song ends by making reference to Romans 8:31–39, which is an absolutely epic portion of Scripture.

What then are we to say about these things? If God is for us,
who is against us? He who did not withhold his own Son, but
gave him up for all of us, will he not with him also give us
everything else? Who will bring any charge against God's elect?

It is God who justifies. Who is to condemn? It is Christ Jesus, who died, yes, who was raised, who is at the right hand of God, who indeed intercedes for us. Who will separate us from the love of Christ? Will hardship, or distress, or persecution, or famine, or nakedness, or peril, or sword?... No, in all these things we are more than conquerors through him who loved us. For I am convinced that neither death, nor life, nor angels, nor rulers, nor things present, nor things to come, nor powers, nor height, nor depth, nor anything else in all creation will be able to separate us from the love of God in Christ Jesus our Lord.

Beautiful, isn't it? Stop and put this book down, and sit with this passage for a few minutes. Read it again slowly.

We are so safe, secure, and loved by Jesus. He has not only forgiven us and made reparation for our sins, but he passionately cares for and loves us. He fights for us. We have nothing to fear, not even the perceived vulnerability of forgiving those who have hurt us. Nothing external can separate us from the love of God.

But we can separate ourselves from his love by our own rebellion toward him; we've all done it. And in my case, my rebellion was my refusal to forgive. Thank God he unveiled my eyes to see that rebellion and sin. It was terrible and I knew it...and I was so grateful to know that I absolutely needed him to die on the cross for my sins because they were ugly, heavy, and serious. I was arrogant, self-righteous, and pompous. *Lord, have mercy on me!* And he did—and he does.

It's Going to Be Okay

Showing mercy and forgiving is tough. It's hard—there's no doubt about that. To relinquish our "rights" for resentment and vengeance makes us feel vulnerable and leaves us concerned that justice will not be served. But the truth is that we are in good hands. We are not relinquishing our "right to resentment" into the hands of those who hurt us. Instead we are entrusting our wounds to the One who fiercely loves us. It's a secure love, the love of our strong, good Father who commands authority and justice. It's the loving care, help, and guidance of the Advocate who protects us and our interests. It's the unstoppable love of our hero and Saviour, Jesus Christ, who will not let anything get in the way of his mercy for us. Each of the Persons of the Trinity uniquely strengthens us with supernatural help, empowering us to be merciful to those who have hurt us. They also give us to the grace to recognize and remember the mercy and love we have received despite our own betrayals, sins, weaknesses, and failures.

Questions for Personal Reflection

1. *Is there anything I'm afraid to forgive? What do I feel I might lose by forgiving?*

2. *How do I feel about entrusting the situation to God's hands? Where am I with believing that God will take care of me and "give me justice"—if not now, surely in heaven?*

3. *How do I see the Father? Who or what is an image or icon for me to better understand my Heavenly Father? Can I trust this Person with my pain and release it in his hands?*

4. *What would change in my heart, if I knew I had the best possible defense lawyer pleading my case?*

5. *What is preventing me from believing that Jesus will go—and has gone—to the ends of the earth to rescue me?*

6. *How does intimately knowing God's goodness and protection allow me to move forward in forgiveness?*

7. *What are the truths that I want to remember from this chapter?*

— ⌒ THREE ⌒ —

Preparing for Forgiveness and Repentance

"For which of you, intending to build a tower, does not first sit
it down and estimate the cost?"
—Luke 14:28

IT WASN'T UNTIL we thought about the possibility of selling our house that we realized, "We can't even think about selling until we do renovations—big time."

Suddenly I was scanning every nook and cranny of the house with someone else's eyes, and in a short time I was very annoyed. *Why had I never noticed how beat up the baseboards were? How could we have put up with that yellow bathroom sink for so long? Wow, we have "Frankenstein flooring": five different floor coverings on 800 square feet of space. An impressive feat in some respects, I suppose. Hmmm, we really need to think about investing in renovations.*

Crazy how it didn't faze me before this. I shouldn't have been surprised, though, as I'm oblivious to balloons and birthday decorations left on the walls weeks after a birthday party. (That actually works out well when you have multiple birthdays in one month—just saying.) I have a propensity to being blind to my own surroundings. If it weren't for the kids' vehement frustration that we have to get our outdoor Christmas decorations down before Easter, I think they might just be ready and waiting for "Christmas in July." It's not that I'm lazy about these things; I simply don't notice them. I'm oblivious.

So the first step in undertaking renovations is realizing they need to happen! Emphasis on "they need to happen." Nobody wants to do renovations! We value the results of renovations, but most of us avoid renovations if we can because we know the process will destroy our living space for weeks or months, cost more than expected, involve more work than anticipated, and cover every surface with dust. In short, to undergo renovations you have to be pretty motivated.

After the macro-decision that renos are needed comes the micro level: sitting down with paper and pen to assess and outline what needs to go, what needs to be fixed, what needs to be added, the cost, the time…everything.

For me forgiveness was like our decision to undergo renovations. At first I was oblivious and blind to the rot in my life until God broke through in answer to my prayer. I saw my life with new eyes and was astounded with the state of affairs. It was beyond obvious, and I had to do something about it. I couldn't stand it any longer.

Just because I was motivated to clean up "the smell and the mess" in my life, don't think I was happy or excited about it. In fact I was scared. I felt fragile, weak, vulnerable, and exposed. The sheer pervasiveness of my sin was overwhelming. Where would I start? How could I face this? Was it pointless even to try? But I couldn't stand it anymore—something had to be done. It was time to call in the professionals.

More Motivation

I was motivated to face my unforgiveness for the sake of my children. Remember the Scripture verses about honouring and dishonouring parents—and how that has a ripple effect on one's own future and one's children's futures? The effect that our own sins have on our families is really pretty easy to spot when you start looking for it. Often the issues you notice in your life are present in your parents' lives, and in their parents' lives, and so on. How prolific is alcoholism through a family's generations? Or sexual abuse? Or infidelity? Or manipulation and control?

So many of my own issues came out of the pain my parents experienced in their own lives—and likely out of the weaknesses of their parents. Sin gets passed down from one generation to the next. I didn't want my children to inherit my garbage, my lack of trust, my abandonment issues, my low self-esteem, and my fears. My biggest concern was my history of anger. I didn't want my kids to be subject to the same poison that had corroded my relationship with my mom. I didn't want that kind of a relationship with my own children, and I certainly didn't want them to be slaves to the anger and bitterness I carried. If I wasn't brave enough to face the chaos of my inner world for my own peace and wholeness, I definitely was for my kids' sake.

If my determination could be portrayed like a movie scene, it would be a bit like Gandalf facing off the Balrog in the Mines of Moria in *The Lord of the Rings*.[8]

Gandalf, the wise and good wizard, stands on the precipice of a chasm, facing an enormous, fearsome evil creature probably a hundred times his size. He strikes his staff on the rock and yells with authority and determination: "You shall not pass!" Gandalf wasn't just fighting off a deadly foe; he was protecting the seven others of "the fellowship of the ring." For the sake of his friends, he would no longer run from the Balrog, but rather confront the creature once and for all.

I felt a little bit like Gandalf. My decision to face the renovation work on my soul was tantamount to standing up against Satan, with my children behind me, facing the tempest of all he was hurling at me and my family with overwhelming smoke, unbelievable stench, blazing fire, and violent winds. I would look behind me at the little faces hanging on to my skirt, turn around and stare him in the eyes, and yell with Gandalf-like focus, "This ends here!"

See, I have set before you today life and prosperity, death and adversity. If you obey the commandments of the LORD your God that I am commanding you today, by loving the LORD your God, walking in his ways, and observing his commandments, decrees, and ordinances, then you shall live and become numerous,

---

8 *The Lord of the Rings: The Fellowship of the Ring*, directed by Peter Jackson (Los Angeles: New Line Cinema, 2001).

and the LORD your God will bless you in the land that you are entering to possess. But if your heart turns away and you do not hear, but are led astray to bow down to other gods and serve them, I declare to you today that you shall perish; you shall not live long in the land that you are crossing the Jordan to enter and possess. I call heaven and earth to witness against you today that I have set before you life and death, blessings and curses. Choose life so that you and your descendants may live, loving the LORD your God, obeying him, and holding fast to him; for that means life to you and length of days, so that you may live in the land that the LORD swore to give to your ancestors, to Abraham, to Isaac, and to Jacob. (Deuteronomy 30:15–20, emphasis added)

The prayer of my heart was, "Yes, Lord, especially for my children and my children's children's sake, right now, right here, I choose life!"

Prepare to Forgive

Choosing life requires thought and planning. Whether it's forgiving or doing household renovations, it is important to do a thorough assessment of the situation.

This was the next step for me coming out of that summer of '97. I knew I needed to forgive and repent, but I also knew the process would be extensive because it was so overdue and so necessary. Just as I planned our renovation work, I literally got out paper and pen and outlined the situation at hand. It took several lengthy sittings with my journal to sort through the closets and junk piles of my heart.

Writing everything out was tremendously cathartic in and of itself. The way I approached it was pretty simple. I identified key relationships in my life where there was pain. These involved people like my parents, other family members, friends, teachers, bullies, and yes, God and myself. For each person I wrote out general and specific areas of hurt. The more specific I was, the better.

I identified hurtful words or actions which had left me convinced I was abandoned, ugly, and rejected. I went back through the whole timeline of my life: through my early married life, university years, high school, grade school, and early childhood. I went as far back in my memory as I could reach, even imagining the situation my parents were in when I was in utero. (What could in utero possibly cover, you may be wondering? It could involve forgiving your parents for the way you were conceived and how they desired—or did not desire—your arrival.) Going this far back, I realized I had to forgive God for allowing me to come into this world from a "destined to fail" relationship.

Prepare to Repent

I reviewed all the things I needed to forgive others for—the things they said and did or what they failed to do, all of which were hurtful. But there's more. I was part of the problem, too. I needed to take inventory of what I had said, done, and failed to do to others as well. I needed to forgive, but I also needed to repent.

So next I went back through the various relationships and circumstances of my life and considered my own sin. I have already shared how the Holy Spirit convicted me of dishonouring my parents and refusing to forgive them. Claiming the right to harbour grudges or resentment was also at the top of my "things to repent of" list. Other big hitters were detraction (speaking badly about another person), judging others, rejecting others, retaliation, and revenge.

Then there was God. I was so angry and bitter toward him that I kept him at arm's length. I didn't fully trust him, and deep down I blamed him for everything painful I had ever experienced.

I had to seriously consider my contributing role in all this. My bad attitudes and actions needed to be exposed and acknowledged. To use the renovation analogy, let's say I discover a huge mold problem in my walls. I become furious about this. I want to blame anything and anyone for it. When the insurance inspectors come to do the assessment, it becomes clear that it is due to our failure to maintain our exhaust fan, which is completely blocked and hasn't been cleaned for well over a decade. If we had taken proper care of the fan, we would not have rotten walls.

But what if I didn't know we were supposed to clean the exhaust fan? Seriously, how's a person supposed to know that kind of stuff?

Maybe super-dads know, but I wouldn't have known. Yes, there were dust bunnies waving at me from the vents of the exhaust fan, but that doesn't mean I would make the connection. Remember? I'm oblivious half the time.

In a similar fashion, I really had no clue about the state of my heart and what I should be doing about it. But thank God, the Holy Spirit answered my prayer and opened my eyes. I finally saw that so much of the rot in my life was due to my own sinfulness.

Get to the Root

This can also be compared to dealing with dandelions in your yard. They are invasive and frustrating. There's no point in pulling out some of the dandelions from your garden, because the ones you didn't pick will just reproduce ten times more! With dandelions, you have to make sure to remove the entire root, because if you don't, in short time another plant will sprout up. If you're going to get rid of dandelions on your property, you've really got to get them all, and get them at the root, or they will just propagate and soon dominate the garden again.

All analogies have their weaknesses, and even though I just said you must get rid of all the dandelions, I want to clarify something. When applying this to forgiveness, I am not saying that you need to dig and snoop and search for every shred of unforgiveness in your life or you'll fail in this process. It is the Holy Spirit who will reveal to you what you need to deal with. Back to the analogy, if he shows you clearly that you have a dandelion problem, then go after those dandelions. If he later makes it clear to you that you have a quack grass problem, then focus in on getting rid of the quack grass as well as you can. The Holy Spirit will prompt you about what you should focus on next.

I find that God is very gentle with us, revealing at teachable moments what he wants us to deal with. Can you imagine if he unveiled everything in our lives that needed a spiritual overhaul all at once? We'd never survive that, and he knows it. He will do it in his time, at his pace, when he knows you are in the appropriate place to respond. (You might not feel like you can respond to it when he surfaces it, but he knows you better than you know yourself, and he will guide you through it one step at a time.)

Lies and Truths

Another thing I found helpful was identifying the lies I was believing and countering those lies with truth.

My experiences led me to believe many lies. One of those lies was abandonment—the sense that I would always end up carrying the burden of a difficult situation alone. This was something that played out for me with teams at work or in the parish. I often felt I was left to do the lion's share of the work alone. I would get so angry and emotional about these situations and find myself muttering, "Again? Really? How come I always get stuck carrying the brunt of the work?"

"How come" indeed! How come? Because I believed it was true! Was it true? Did I really always get stuck with the burden of situations? Or was it a skewed perception I had of reality, a particular coloured lens through which I was looking at life because of my unforgiveness toward my parents? I needed to forgive my parents for leaving me with the burden of their failed relationship. But I also needed to expose and counter the lie that was in play.

The lie was that I alone was left to deal with the repercussions of their relationship. The truth was that no one expected this of me. The truth was that I was not alone in this situation. I had my mom, God gave me my new dad when I was four years old, and he blessed me with a loving and large extended family that was always nearby. And the truth about God himself in all of this was that he never left me to deal with the messy situation on my own. He was always with me.

Where can I go from your spirit? Or where can I flee from your presence? If I ascend to heaven, you are there; if I make my bed in Sheol, you are there. If I take the wings of the morning and settle at the farthest limits of the sea, even there your hand shall lead me, and your right hand shall hold me fast. (Psalm 139:7–10)

I can't emphasise enough the absolute necessity of the inspiration of the Holy Spirit in all of this self-reflection. Ultimately the entire renovation work was his work in me. It wasn't until the Holy Spirit opened my eyes that I was able to understand my situation. He guided my reflections so I could recognize the pain, the sin, the lies, and the truths. "When the Spirit of truth comes, he will guide you into all the truth" (John 16:13b).

The Holy Spirit also emboldened me with courage, and this was key as I examined myself. Without the Holy Spirit's presence, I would have been too afraid to deal with my issues. Scripture tells us that the Holy Spirit is our Comforter, and how appropriate this attribute was when I was flooded with emotions of anger or sadness. Here again the Holy Spirit was my star defense lawyer, my Paraclete. I could be confident following his expert guidance, leading, and inspiration.

Renovation Recap

As you prepare for your own renovations of the heart, here is a summary of practical pointers I recommend.

Journal—You're going to be doing a lot of writing, my friend! (If you're worried about anyone peeking, you could always get one of those snazzy "preteen" diaries that come with a built-in lock and key on the cover!)

Pray—Ask the Holy Spirit for the grace to understand the situation, the comfort of his presence there, and the courage to be merciful.

Identify—Name each person you need to forgive.

List—Write down every hurtful interaction, every mean thing that was said, and all the ways they failed you. Write everything you hold against them in your heart of hearts. List every hurt that you need to release into God's hands. Keep going until you've listed everything you can think of. Don't worry about missing something. If you are doing this sincerely, in a spirit of prayer and obedience to God's call to forgiveness, he will reveal all that's important right now. This step might take you a couple of sittings to do, so be patient.

Forgive yourself—Don't be surprised if you discover you are burdened with regret for past mistakes you've made. Make a list of the regrets the Holy Spirit brings to the surface. Note: Shame is another thing. You may feel deep shame—a sense of being worthless and wretched—even when you have not personally done anything wrong. If your innocence has been violated in some way, you may feel deeply ashamed of what has happened, even though it was not in any way your fault. But regardless of whether you deserve to feel guilty or not, God wants you to be free.

"Forgive" God[9]—You might blame God for things that happened (or didn't happen). List those things too, so you can release your resentment toward him.

Repent—Look at everything you've listed so far, the people and the circumstances, and ask the Holy Spirit to enlighten you about your own sin related to these situations.

List lies and truths—Create two columns, one entitled "lies" and the other "truths." What are the lies you've bought into in light of your life's experiences? What is the truth God would want you to believe in response to those lies?

Thank God—Thank God for the grace to make this examination of your life. Ask for the grace to truly forgive and repent, or at least to be willing to be willing to forgive and repent.

Questions for Personal Reflection

1. *How is God inviting me to a deeper forgiveness and release from the painful issues of my life?*

2. *Am I ready to do the preparatory work necessary to understand my heart and its hurts?*

3. *Who has hurt me? List all the ways and circumstances involved as thoroughly as necessary.*

4. *What personal regrets do I have for which I need to forgive myself?*

5. *What resentments might I have toward God?*

6. *What lies have influenced my thinking in all of this?*

7. *What truths counter each of those lies?*

---

9 We can't really forgive God, since forgiveness implies that someone has sinned against us, which obviously God cannot do. However, it can be helpful for our healing to acknowledge any resentment we might feel toward God and let that go by expressing our forgiveness to him.

— ∞ **FOUR** ∞ —

Praying through Forgiveness
and Repentance

*"Therefore confess your sins to one another, and pray for one another,
so that you may be healed. The prayer of the righteous is
powerful and effective."*
—James 5:16

ONCE YOU'VE SCOPED out the plans and budget for your
renovations, it's time to bring in the professionals. Forgiveness is not
a "do it yourself" project. For forgiveness to take effect, there is a
social dimension. Words have to be communicated to another person,
expressing the decision to forgive. Healing doesn't happen in private.

That's a strong statement, so let me back it up.

Who could deny the effectiveness of the twelve-step program for
addiction recovery as outlined in Alcoholics Anonymous (AA)? Let's
look at the first five steps.

1. *Admit we were powerless over alcohol—that our lives had
   become unmanageable.*
2. *Believe that a Power greater than ourselves could restore us
   to sanity.*
3. *Make a decision to turn our will and our lives over to the
   care of God as we understood him.*
4. *Make a searching and fearless moral inventory of ourselves.*
5. *Admit to God, to ourselves, and to another human being the
   exact nature of our wrongs.*

Step five is what catches my attention: admit to God, ourselves, and someone else! Yikes! Notice that in the journey I've recounted to you so far, I have gone through the first four steps, but I have not yet taken the big leap of step five.

Why do we have to come out of the private realm of our own thoughts and heart and speak to another human being? Because disclosing the pain, regret, resentment, and bitterness to someone else somehow undoes the power it has over us just by admitting it. The words of Jesus ring true: "You will know the truth, and the truth will make you free" (John 8:32).

Admitting your failings to someone else makes the sin more concrete. It's a humbling thing to do, so telling another person indicates how serious we are about changing our life. It puts us in a place of accountability. We think, *Now that my friend knows about this problem, she will be watching me more closely! I'd better be careful to stick to my decision.*

The Catholic Church knows the power of these principles better than anyone. The sacrament of Reconciliation is a sure source of help in the natural scope of things, as well as in the supernatural.

This chapter addresses how to forgive someone else, and confession is a key component of this. For forgiveness and healing to happen well, we need to admit our need to forgive to another person, and a priest is a terrific choice. And one aspect of forgiving is confessing your resentment and bitterness to God in the sacrament of reconciliation.

Many people's reaction at the thought of going to confession is resistance. "No, thank you! I don't need to confess my sins to a priest! Why should I have to?" I'm sure we can all relate.

As a convert to the Catholic Church, the idea of going to confession sounded like a really awkward thing to do. To my amazement the Catholics I met during my time of preparation didn't seem to feel all that awkward about it. They talked about it so naturally and comfortably, and it seemed to be a pretty positive experience for them.

When I talked to our parish pastor, Fr. Clair, about it, he told me that while the practice of regularly going to confession has been increasingly declining since the 1960s, the demand for psychological counselling has dramatically increased. On a natural level, people need somewhere to talk about the deepest things affecting their lives; and they need to talk to a professional about them.

In the confessional we receive so much. It's a place to expose our weaknesses and failures to someone else as an aid to our healing, but we also receive wise counsel on how to move forward and amend our life. And the greatest thing we receive in confession is absolution!

When Catholics confess their sins in the sacrament of reconciliation with contrition—that is, with sincere sorrow for what they have done or failed to do and a desire not to sin again—they receive absolution. Absolution is incredible. Here's what happens.

The priest, acting *in persona Christi* (that is, representing Christ), assures us that those sins have been forgiven. It's amazing. I have never gone to confession, heard these words prayed over me, and not been moved to tears.

> *God, the Father of mercies, through the death and the resurrection of his Son has reconciled the world to himself and sent the Holy Spirit among us for the forgiveness of sins; through the ministry of the Church may God give you pardon and peace, and I absolve you from your sins in the name of the Father, and of the Son, and of the Holy Spirit.*

I don't think I get choked up because the words are particularly poetic. Instead these words are truth and power, spoken by a man who has the authority to say them! When the priest speaks these words, I am actually receiving God's forgiveness and the supernatural grace to help me reform my ways. The most awkward part of confession is coming out of the confessional and facing all the impatient and nervous people waiting in line, especially when your eyes are puffy and your lips are still quivering.

Confession is such a gift, because it gives us the assurance that we've been absolved of our sins. If I just pray and ask God to forgive me in private, all I can do is hope that he hears me and forgives me.

But the sacrament of reconciliation is a concrete anchor of hope. There I am assured by a professional that God has heard my sins and forgiven me; it is incredibly freeing.

Jesus gave his disciples the authority to forgive sins, and the Church teaches that the same authority is passed on to Catholic priests when they are ordained. "When he had said this, he breathed on them and said to them, 'Receive the Holy Spirit. If you forgive the sins of any, they are forgiven them; if you retain the sins of any, they are retained'" (John 20:22–23).

This is sacred stuff!

One of the greatest joys in CCO's work on campus is when our missionaries or student leaders bring someone to confession for the first time in a long time. Usually it's their "second confession." That is, the last time they went was at their first reconciliation. It is such a privilege to witness the whole encounter. So many approach the sacrament like the Prodigal Son coming home to the Father: timid, ashamed, unsure if they will face rejection but ready to change the direction their life is headed. You can see the change in them as soon as they leave the confessional. They just look different. You can see it in their eyes, in how they walk, and in their composure.

Praying through Forgiveness

Forgiveness is best done in the context of prayer. I suppose you could forgive by praying on your own, but based on the solid advice from AA and from personal experience, the most effective way to pray through forgiveness is aloud with another human being. This person is with you during this time as a witness to your prayers, and he or she is there to pray for you and support you as you release people and pain into God's hands.

Bringing all of this to the sacrament of reconciliation is amazing and necessary for healing. But by praying through forgiveness with someone else before you get to the confessional, you can do some valuable preliminary work to prepare your heart. By forgiving and releasing people who have hurt you before going to confession, you can focus on what you need to repent of in the sacrament.

I give this advice because I find it is tempting in the confessional to slip into confessing everybody else's sins against me. "Father, I want to confess that I'm really mad that so-and-so did this to me. And then they even did this, and then that!" As you can see, so-and-so's sins can get much more airtime in the confessional than my own. I suggest we keep our confessions first and foremost focused on our own need to repent.

Praying through forgiveness involves an extended period of time, in a private place, to pray with a trusted person through the relationships and incidents you need to forgive and release to God. It starts with a brief opening prayer to welcome God in your midst and invite the Holy Spirit to lead your time together. You share and talk though all the journaling you did, and then you pray. Your friend prays for you as you pray aloud and specifically forgive each person's failures toward you.

It might seem as though you are wading through a long grocery list of items, but that's okay. Your prayers might sounds something like this:

> *Lord, I want to forgive my brother for rejecting me so many times, especially that first experience when he refused to let me go with him to the lake. I also forgive my brother all the times he called me names like "stupid," "ugly," and "idiot." I forgive my brother for saying these things that led me to believe they might be true. I forgive my brother for making fun of me in front of his friends and making me cry. I forgive him for all these things, and I release him from the right I feel I have to hate him for it. I choose not to hold these things against him any longer.*

Verbalizing forgiveness like this is a concrete way to prove to yourself and the Lord that you are choosing to forgive and release these people. You might pray through forgiveness with a trusted friend, a spiritual director, a Christian counselor, or a prayer ministry team. If you know a priest who is willing to do prayer ministry (the process of being led in prayer by another person to minister to an intimate area of your life) with you through all the areas of forgiveness you've prepared, you are blessed indeed, because priests do not always have that kind of time available.

When you work through forgiveness in the context of prayer ministry, you can give yourself as much time as you need. I recommend giving yourself at least an hour or two. That might sound daunting, but you'll be surprised how quickly time flies when you pray this way.

I benefitted from this kind of prayer ministry one July evening in 1997. I was at the home of a married couple who were gifted in counselling. Their little children were tucked into bed for the night, and we had the whole evening to pray.

We sat on three comfortable chairs in the living room, with Bibles close at hand, my journal on my lap, and a box of tissues at my feet. We walked through my list prayerfully and thoughtfully. They helped me pray through and verbalize my forgiveness and release my pain to God. They gently reminded me to make sure I said, "I forgive," and "I choose to release," as I shared these wounds aloud. Sometimes they encouraged me to dig a little deeper and be more specific about what I was forgiving.

For example, while forgiving family members of some early experiences, one of them said, "I think you also need to repent of believing and hanging on to the lie that you are ugly." It was true. I believed that I was ugly, and I believed that everyone else thought I was ugly, too. I needed to forgive people for those painful comments, but I also needed to repent of believing that lie. If life was a movie, the script that had been written for me was that I was ugly and abandoned. I had lived my whole life out of that script. I believed it. I lived it and breathed it. My friends reminded me that I needed to repent of believing this lie as well as all the times I was jealous of others who were beautiful.

This is just a little snippet of what prayer ministry looks like. I went through my list methodically and prayerfully. We took our time to do all the "weeding" that was required. It was pretty extensive, I will admit, but I was really ready. I had given God permission to reveal my sin to me, and when he did, I was determined to do whatever it would take to clean it up.

About a week or so later, I met with my parish priest to receive the sacrament of reconciliation. I told the priest about this massive forgiveness extravaganza. I told him, in broad strokes, about my issues and the people (including myself and God) whom I had forgiven during prayer ministry.

But for the most part, my confession consisted of owning up to the serious sins I had committed in my anger and pain (harbouring bitterness, dishonouring, judging, believing lies, denying how God valued me, and refusing to forgive). And those were just my "bad attitude sins"! I had another long list of "bad action sins"—how I had deliberately lashed out in mean ways and with mean words.

Since I knew this wasn't going to be a quick confession, I scheduled a time to meet with the priest. Although it wasn't short, it wasn't that long either—maybe half an hour at the most.

When I heard the words of absolution that day, I wasn't filled with excitement or joy. Instead what I felt was simply peace. I was at rest. My soul was refreshed. I hadn't merely heard those beautiful words—I had *received* them.

> *...through the ministry of the Church may God give you pardon and peace, and I absolve you from your sins...*

What happened that summer was nothing short of a miracle. My Lenten prayer was being answered. A year or so earlier I had no clue how God could possibly come up with something that would make me feel a sense of my sinfulness. He didn't have to invent something; it was all there, ripe for the picking. By God's grace I received a good long look into my rot and sin, and oh, what joy to know that I indeed needed a mighty Saviour!

Questions for Personal Reflection

1. *How might the fruits and effectiveness of forgiving be different for me and my healing if I do it with the help of someone else instead of privately by myself?*

2. *How do I feel about admitting my resentment and pain to another person?*

3. *Who could I approach to pray with me as I work through the areas I need to forgive and release to God?*

4. *What might be the best opportunity for me to receive the sacrament of reconciliation?*

— ☙ **FIVE** ❧ —

After the Sacrament of Reconciliation

"If it is possible, so far as it depends on you, live peaceably with all."
—*Romans 12:18*

THE SACRAMENT OF reconciliation is an encounter with God himself and his mercy. Its aim is our salvation—with a catch! We have an obligation to cooperate with those graces through penance and by seeking reconciliation and peace. The goal is conversion and reform of life.

Here's what the *Catechism of the Catholic Church* says about penance:

> *Many sins wrong our neighbor. One must do what is possible in order to repair the harm (e.g., return stolen goods, restore the reputation of someone slandered, pay compensation for injuries). Simple justice requires as much. But sin also injures and weakens the sinner himself, as well as his relationships with God and neighbor. Absolution takes away sin, but it does not remedy all the disorders sin has caused. Raised up from sin, the sinner must still recover his full spiritual health by doing something more to make amends for the sin: he must "make satisfaction for" or "expiate" his sins. This satisfaction is also called "penance." (CCC, 1459)*

Have you noticed that penance is something the priest asks you to do as soon as possible—preferably immediately after confession?

He's not just being impatient or picky. That's what the Church expects—that we do our penance as soon as possible. Doing it right away proves our contrition and ensures that we don't forget to do it.

Penance is our response to God's mercy. It is a concrete act by which we demonstrate to God our sorrow for what we've done and our attempt to make (at least some) amends for it. The concrete nature of penance acts to counteract our habits. Penance is comforting in that it gives us the chance to do something for God in gratitude. When someone helps you out of a desperate situation, you want to buy that person a gift or do something to show your gratitude. If you run out of gas on the highway and a perfect stranger emerges on the scene and takes care of all of your needs, you can't thank him or her enough! That's a bit of what penance is like. Penance proves our sorrow and gratitude, and it helps us takes practical steps to reform our life.

Penance has that public social dimension, too, which is connected to the power of the fifth step in AA—"admitting to another human being." Oftentimes penances are prayers that we pray in the pew right after confession. The public part of this is that everyone can see you're praying. Sometimes the priest will give you a more concrete penance to make amends directly related to the issue.

Whenever I think of penance, my mind always goes to the "penance scene" from the movie *The Mission*.[10] Leading up to this scene Rodrigo Mendoza, slave trader and mercenary, has recently killed his brother (for his adulterous relationship with Rodrigo's wife). He is overwhelmed with feelings of betrayal, pain, and deep regret—because he loved his brother and his wife.

Fr. Gabriel, a missionary to the remote tribal Guaraní people—the same people Mendoza captured for the slave trade—comes to visit him in jail. Fr. Gabriel is concerned for his soul. Rodrigo, very aware of his many sins, has lost all hope of redemption. When Fr. Gabriel challenges him to repentance and reconciliation with God, Mendoza replies, "There is no penance hard enough for me."

Fr. Gabriel takes him up on the challenge in order to fight for

---

10 *The Mission*, directed by Roland Joffe (Burbank, Calif.: Warner Bros, 1986).

his soul. He knows Rodrigo needs penance for healing and in order to prove his deep regret and sorrow. In the famous "penance scene," the Jesuit missionaries lead Mendoza up the treacherous cliff face of some mountainous waterfalls in the Amazon rainforest. If that wasn't dangerous enough, Mendoza is dragging behind him a huge net filled with the trappings of his past life—armour, swords, shields, and weapons. The journey up and over the waterfall to the Guaraní is gruelling and painful for the Jesuits to watch, but Fr. Gabriel knows Mendoza needs to prove his remorse to God.

When they finally get to the San Miguel mission where the Guaraní are, there is a scrum. The Guaraní recognize him as the slave trader, and one of the warriors rushes over to him with a blade in his hand and a fierce look in his eyes. Rodrigo knows the warrior has every right to kill him right there. Rodrigo also has absolutely no energy to defend himself; there's nothing left in him. He's used every ounce of his strength to get himself to the mission. He lays at the feet of the warriors—guilty, powerless, and vulnerable. He is a broken man.

The Guaraní chief, seeing the net filled with armour and the pitiful state of Mendoza, realizes what is happening. He barks a command at the warrior, who immediately raises his blade. Mendoza squeezes his eyes shut, only to hear the sounds of the rope being sawed, followed by the sweet relief of his burden being cast off his shoulders and tumbling down the mountainside. He collapses in tears of amazement, joy, gratitude, release, reconciliation, and restoration. He has made his peace with God and the Guaraní. He is a new creation.

Penance as illustrated here is a source of grace to help the healing of repentance take effect. Confession is often called the sacrament of penance or the sacrament of reconciliation. In this healing sacrament we are reconciled to God, but his intent is for us also to be at peace with the people in our relationships.

The Importance of Reconciliation

Do not repay anyone evil for evil, but take thought for what is noble in the sight of all. If it is possible, so far as it depends on you, live peaceably with all. (Romans 12:17–18)

As God's chosen ones, holy and beloved, clothe yourselves with compassion, kindness, humility, meekness, and patience. Bear with one another and, if anyone has a complaint against another, forgive each other; just as the Lord has forgiven you, so you also must forgive. (Colossians 3:12–13)

Confession allows us to make our peace with God and empowers us to make our peace with our neighbour (inasmuch as we can). Efforts to "bear with one another," "live in peace with one another," and "forgive one another" often end up being "bonus penance" (i.e., penance the priest didn't give us in the confessional). Decisions to be loving and live peacefully prove our desire to "be merciful, just as your Father is merciful" (Luke 6:36).

Reconciling with someone who has hurt you or with someone you have hurt is not easy. It's the kind of thing most of us want to avoid. It's embarrassing, uncomfortable, humiliating, and delicate. You don't know how the other person is going to respond emotionally. Will he or she be angry, defensive, hurt? Will he or she cry, yell, or be silent? Will the person push back or turn away?

Something we haven't talked about yet is directly forgiving those who have offended you and letting them know you forgive them. Depending on the relationship and situation, this might be absolutely necessary or perhaps not possible.

Sometimes direct reconciliation isn't possible (because the person is deceased or dangerous), or it isn't a good idea (because the person is not emotionally stable or mature enough to recognize his or her fault and have empathy). In some cases it might not even be wise to re-engage with a person because the relationship is dangerous or toxic. This is when your priest, a spiritual director, or a counsellor can help you discern if and how you should forgive the people who have hurt you.

But for most relationships there is a possibility for reconciliation, sometimes through a deep heart-to-heart airing of the situation. Sometimes a small gesture or a shared moment is enough to communicate everything.

Full disclosure: The way I tend to approach reconciliation is that I want all the benefits of it—but not the work of it. I don't know what it is about uncomfortable, confrontational debate that doesn't seem to attract me. I must be weird, I guess!

God, in his kindness to me, knowing how weak I am, took his time to bring me into this phase of actually reconciling with others. The first phase of God's overhaul on my heart was when I went for prayer ministry and then to confession. Knowing my steep learning curve, he let that first part soak in—or as I like to put it, "let it marinate"—for a few months.

Reconciling with My Mother

One wintery day the Lord challenged me during my prayer time about actually reconciling with my mom. While I had forgiven her "officially" and had repented of my sin toward her in the confessional, I never felt prompted to approach her directly about all this forgiveness stuff—until now.

This idea came as a huge shock. I immediately panicked because I hadn't even told my mom about any of my inner healing journey. I knew God's challenge to me to approach her was "right and just," but my pride was freaking out. So awkward!

The next day in prayer I said, "Okay, God, fine, I hear you. I should deal with Mom. You're right. I guess I should get everything out in the open and tell her all the ways she hurt me and how I've forgiven her."

And I felt the Lord say back to me, loud and clear, "NO!"

He impressed upon me how that approach—reviewing all the ways she hurt me—is a spiritualized form of retaliation. Of course it would be done in a pious way: "You know, I've really prayed about this, and I just want you to know I forgive you for…." The whole thing is simply dripping with self-righteousness and revenge. (I'd actually been on the receiving end of something like that before. I had a friend visit me with a clipboard and a piece of paper on which she had written a long list of things to "forgive me for.")

I felt the Lord was asking me to phone my mom (I was in Ottawa, and she was in Saskatchewan) and tell her all the ways I had failed her. I was not excited about doing this; it was very humbling and humiliating for me. But by God's grace I had the courage and strength to do it. And it was surprisingly a very good conversation!

A beautiful fruit from reconciling with my mom was that she mailed me a letter a couple of weeks later. In the letter she listed her regrets and failures toward me, which was very healing. These were the very things I initially had contemplated sharing with her: "Mom, I want you to know I forgive you for..." What a difference to have her repent of that list rather than me using the list to flood her with shame!

There are times to confront others about the hurt they've caused, but I would recommend prayerful discernment first as well as consulting your priest, a spiritual director, or close mature Christian friends about whether direct confrontation is the necessary course of action.

The Lord blessed my docility. I have a much better and tender relationship with my mom. It is as though forgiving and repenting of judging her released her and enabled her to react differently to me. But it was not easy to make that phone call. I really struggled to get my heart in the right place, because I didn't want to call her. My pride was freaking out. It was embarrassing, it was humbling, and it was awkward.

I'll give you a little tip, though. I wrote out a script of what I planned to say. I knew if I didn't write it out, I would trip over my words, forget something, or ramble on in my nervousness. It actually worked out better than I expected, and she never suspected that I was reading my words—until now. (Yes indeed, she is very aware that I'm writing about this journey—and she has graciously given this book her blessing.)

Even though I had a script to follow for that phone conversation, it was still one of the hardest things I've ever done. It was ultimately a battle with my own pride. It was an opportunity to live out the forgiveness I had professed to God by concretely speaking to Mom. I was able to practice forgiveness in the sense of releasing Mom from any "rights" I may have thought I had to exact vengeance by admitting my own failures rather than listing hers.

The Lord had been teaching me to move beyond my wounds,

pain, and sin. He was now discipling me to take my eyes off myself and start thinking about others. How could I pursue reconciliation—not for my own benefit or peace of mind, but for the sake of the relationship—and bring healing to the other person? In my woundedness and immaturity, I could have easily wielded truth under the guise of reconciliation to hurt Mom. That was my first impulse. But somehow by God's grace, I understood that he wanted me to repent rather than accuse and condemn.

Questions for Personal Reflection

1. *Considering my past reflections from previous chapters, is the Lord inviting me to do something more about those areas now that I've gone to confession? (What might my priest or spiritual director say?)*

2. *Matthew 5:23–24 says, "If you remember that your brother or sister has something against you…be reconciled." Who might be holding something against me?*

3. *Considering all the relationships that come to mind, who do I sense the Lord is inviting me to reconcile with?*

4. *How do I feel about reconciling with each of these people? What apprehensions do I have?*

5. *What truths might incite me to have courage to give God permission to help me embrace the call to reconciliation?*

6. *I will ask the Holy Spirit, "How should I proceed at this time to reconcile this relationship?" A priest, spiritual director, or close friend can help me in this discernment.*

— ⌒ SIX ⌒ —
Deeper and Weaker

"For when I am weak then I am strong."
—*2 Corinthians 12:10*

DO YOU FIND it easy to apologize? I know my kids find it pretty hard.

Have you ever tried to get a child to apologize after a family fight? My husband and I firmly believe that ability to say you're sorry is an important life lesson, but it's not easy to teach. These "life lessons" go a little something like this:

Me: "Say 'sorry' to your brother."

Kid: (grunt)

Me: "Excuse me? Say 'sorry'!"

Kid: (mutters) "Sorry."

Me: "I can't hear you."

Kid: (yells) "SORRY!"

Me: "Say it like you mean it."

Kid: (sarcastically) "*Sorry.*"

Me: "Try that again."

Kid: (angrily) "SORRRRRy."

Me: "That's not the tone of voice I'm looking for...."

Kid: (whining) "Soar–eeeee."

Me: "You're not leaving here until you say 'sorry' properly."

Kid: (impatiently) "Sorry already...sorry sorry sorry sorry...."

These sorts of conversations can go on for a very long time, especially if your child is a very good actor.

One of our children really struggled with his pride when it came to admitting failure and saying "sorry." At least an hour or more after any given fight, he would approach us reluctantly and mutter, "S" (which implied he was saying "sorry"—his pride refused to let him say the actual word).

We didn't really mind, because this was huge progress. Previously some time after a confrontation, he would slip a paper under our door. Can you guess what was written on the paper? "S."

We tried to teach another one of our children to say sorry. Her response? "I too tired to say 'sorry.'" Well, she was three.

Maybe you feel too tired and too weak to say "sorry" or to forgive. It's a lot of work to face everything.

St. Thérèse is a great role model for us in this area. She rejoiced in her weakness. She knew that being little, helpless, weak, and pathetic was a great opportunity for God to make up in her what she was lacking. In this way he could be her superhero and save her.

If you find that you just don't have what it takes to be courageous, virtuous, or generous enough to forgive, it's okay. You can, like St. Thérèse, be confident that God the Father, Son, and Holy Spirit will help you face your weakness, fear, and inability. The Scriptures tell us: "My grace is sufficient for you, for power is made perfect in weakness" (2 Corinthians 12:9).

Deep Clean

It's also difficult to get kids to do their chores, especially when it's time for a Saturday "deep clean." In our house that means getting rid of all the dust bunnies under the beds and all the greeblies in the corners. ("Greeblies" is a word I invented for random, crunchy, nasty, little bits that you might sweep up off the floor or vacuum out of kitchen drawers. If you like the word, please indulge in its use, just please note that I do claim copyright on it.)

Spiritually, in the late 1990s I was definitely ready for a deep clean. I remember hearing a talk given by Patti Mansfield in 1996. Patti was one of the handful of students to be present at the first eruption of the Catholic Charismatic Renewal when the Holy Spirit manifested himself in an adoration chapel at Duquesne University in

1967. In her talk Patti exhorted us to pray a dangerous prayer: "Lord, invade my privacy."

She shared the story of how she was hosting a bishop at her home during a conference, and how she had taken great care to immaculately clean the main floor of the house, where the guest room was situated. Martha Stewart had nothing on her! Everything looked amazing and coordinated—a model of good housekeeping. After a couple of days, the bishop said, "Patti, your home is so beautiful, but I've only seen this level of the house. I'd love to see the rest; would you mind showing me around?"

She swallowed hard and said, "Now?"

"Why yes, now. Why not?" said the bishop. She then proceeded to lead the bishop up the stairs to the second level. One room after the other she opened the door to show the bishop bedrooms of bedlam. Here she had thrown everything she had decluttered from the main floor. She felt so exposed and humiliated. Her deep clean was only one floor deep.

The Lord used this experience to speak to her heart about her spiritual life, which appeared to be in order in the eyes of other people. But he wanted her to give him permission to do a full deep clean—to deal with all of her mess, especially those areas she wanted to keep private and hidden from him! And so she responded to his invitation and prayed, "Lord, invade my privacy."

I was completely struck by her story. I had spent my whole spiritual life keeping God at arm's length, limiting what I would allow him to ask of me or meddle in. Could I really give God permission like that? Could I invite him to invade my privacy and have permission and access to anything in my life that he wanted to deal with? I was at once both drawn to his light and scared of my chaos. *If I do this, I will be vulnerable. He will probably take this opportunity to embarrass and humiliate me in front of others. How can I trust him with this sort of access?* I was aware that this was an invitation. God had truly honoured the limitations I had placed on access to the rooms of my heart.

I was intrigued by Patti—her genuine joy and freedom was unmistakable. I wanted what she had. I truly wanted to experience that joy and freedom in my relationship with God. My desire for more was fortunately stronger than my fear of what God might do to me (by just a smidgen). So, I sincerely prayed Patti's prayer: "Lord, invade my privacy." I mentally imagined my heart like a three-story home. I imagined myself flinging open every door of every room, every door of every closet and cupboard.

"Lord, invade my privacy. I give you total access. P.S. Please be gentle. Thanks." I prayed this prayer in November 1996, and that's what gave God permission to do all the deep cleaning he started the summer of 1997 when he first opened my eyes to my bitterness and unforgiveness. I believe this powerful prayer catalyzed my reconciliation with my mom.

The value of this experience inspired me to pray all the more fervently, "Yes, Lord, invade my privacy." I began to perceive this spiritual deep clean a bit like purgatory—or at least as a preparation to expedite purgatory.[11]

All who die in God's grace and friendship, but still imperfectly purified, are indeed assured of their eternal salvation; but after death they undergo purification, so as to achieve the holiness necessary to enter the joy of heaven. (CCC, 1030)

Purgatory is a hard concept for some people to understand, especially converts from Protestant backgrounds like myself. Being a hopeless romantic, I have to admit that reflecting on Cinderella helped me to get a handle on it.

Although Cinderella was invited to the ball and desired to go, she simply was in no shape to go to such an esteemed event at the palace—certainly not in a ripped dress with her hair looking like that! You know the story.

Purgatory, in my childlike estimation, is perhaps like the work of the fairy godmother. She restored Cinderella with beautiful hair, a stunning gown, and of course, glass slippers—all of which reflected her true dignity and destiny. It's almost as though the fairy

---

11 Purgatory in Catholic teaching is an intermediary state for souls which die in a state of grace but need cleansing and healing to be ready for heaven.

godmother had read St. Paul: "Everything old has passed away; see, everything has become new!" (2 Corinthians 5:17).

Yes, in a "girlie-girl" way, I like to think of purgatory as getting the ultimate and lasting makeover. God spares no expense and has the "top professionals" working to make you the best version of yourself so you finally are ready for the One who created you to be with him forever.

I'm sure theologians would cringe at that explanation of purgatory, but then I also highly doubt many of them have ever had a makeover, either! My analogy might give the impression that purgatory is a delightful experience. Well, I don't know if anyone can say for a fact whether purgatory is painful or not, but I can tell you I am not assuming it is pleasant. Have you ever had your eyebrows waxed? Ouch!

I imagine purgatory as a supernatural deep clean for my heart! I imagine that the Lord will expose all the rotten, unfinished, and ignored areas of my life. I imagine him unveiling everything I've ever done and all the implications of my actions, judgements, and failures. I imagine him saying to me: "Do you realize what your choices did to these people? Did you know that when you failed to do the right thing, this happened?" I imagine truly, deeply understanding my failures with deep regret and profound empathy for all whom I have hurt.

This was my perspective and motivation when I invited God to invade my privacy. If I'm going to have to come to terms with my weaknesses and failures no matter what, then I might as well let God start doing his thing sooner rather than later. I don't want to spend any more time in purgatory, away from full union with God in heaven, than is necessary. "Bring it on! Lord, invade my privacy. What do you want to clean up next?"

Lent 1998 came on the heels of my reconciliation with my mom. This Lent I definitely had a much deeper understanding of my failures and need for a Saviour. I wanted to let God continue his purging in my life, so throughout those six weeks I invited him to reveal to me anyone and everyone I had hurt. I reflected on what Jesus said in Matthew's Gospel:

So when you are offering your gift at the altar, if you remember that your brother or sister has something against you, leave your

*gift there before the altar and go; first be reconciled to your brother
or sister, and then come and offer your gift. (Matthew 5:23–24)*

Day by day, little by little, during my prayer time the Lord would
bring certain people to mind, and with the Holy Spirit's help, I would
reflect on those relationships and examine how they were damaged.
What was my part in it? How had I caused hurt by my actions and
omissions?

I took these reflections from prayer to the confessional and then
to my computer.

This might seem a bit cowardly, but I reached out to these people
through the written word, by mail or e-mail. Writing letters was a
practical decision initially since everyone I knew was three thousand
kilometres away and I couldn't exactly get together for coffee with
them. I also felt (or maybe I justified in my mind) that a letter gave
people the freedom to receive my message and respond, if they so
desired, in their own time without me expecting a reaction on the spot.

Here's a sample of one of those messages:

Dear Frank,

*I hope you are well. I know it's been a while since you've heard
from me. We have been in Ottawa for about a year now.*

Hey, there's something I wanted to say to you.

I need to apologize for how I have treated you.

*I cringe thinking about how many times I have talked to you
in a sarcastic, rude way. I guess I thought I was being funny or
something, but I wasn't. It was immature and mean-spirited of
me. I am so sorry for the things I've said to you and how I said
them.*

*I am not asking you for a response, I'm really not. I just want
to let you know that, by God's grace, I have finally clued in
to how I treated you, and I want you to know that I regret it
because you are a friend, a good person, and you didn't deserve
to be treated like that.*

Sincerely,

Angèle

I was amazed at how gracious these folks were toward me. Some were appreciative that I admitted my failures in their regard. They had been offended, and they appreciated my reaching out. Others assured me that, even though I thought I had hurt them, they were not hurt. To my surprise (and relief), none of these apologies escalated into larger conflicts or rejection.

There were, however, people who came to mind during this time with whom I did not sense the Lord was inviting me to engage in conversation. These particular relationships were unhealthy, and it likely would have been detrimental to open things up again.

But it was satisfying and a blessing to reconcile with the dozen or so people God did invite me to approach. It was so rewarding that I found myself increasingly willing to follow the Holy Spirit's promptings. I was compelled by the love of Christ to reconcile with others and prepare my heart for him and for heaven. Every day my prayer was "Lord, what else do you want to me do? With whom else do I need to make things right?"

By the end of Lent that year, my conscience was clear (at least for the time being.) The rooms were cleaned, every nook and cranny swept. It was a lot of work, but it was worth it. Fresh air and freedom were the result.

Be Prepared for the Bridegroom

Another Scripture passage that inspired me to prepare my heart for the Lord was the Parable of the Foolish Bridesmaids:

> "Then the kingdom of heaven will be like this. Ten bridesmaids took their lamps and went to meet the bridegroom. Five of them were foolish, and five were wise. When the foolish took their lamps, they took no oil with them; but the wise took flasks of oil with their lamps. As the bridegroom was delayed, all of them became drowsy and slept. But at midnight there was a shout, 'Look! Here is the bridegroom! Come out to meet him.' Then all those bridesmaids got up and trimmed their lamps. The foolish said to the wise, 'Give us some of your oil, for our lamps are going out.' But the wise replied, 'No! there will not be enough

for you and for us; you had better go to the dealers and buy some for yourselves.' And while they went to buy it, the bridegroom came, and those who were ready went with him into the wedding banquet; and the door was shut. Later the other bridesmaids came also, saying, 'Lord, lord, open to us.' But he replied, 'Truly I tell you, I do not know you.' Keep awake therefore, for you know neither the day nor the hour." (Matthew 25:1–13)

I truly heard the Lord's admonition in these words; I wanted to be found ready, for love of him. I wanted to be prepared, ready and waiting, as a bride waits for her bridegroom. Incidentally the Lord did an amazing thing for me during the last week of that Lent related to this theme. Besides doing all this repenting and soul-searching during Lent, my husband, André, and I were doing something else that was not insignificant. We felt called to fast (on liquids only) for forty days that Lent.

I know—that's really radical. We felt called to do this as a way to pray for the world, to pray for conversions. As CCO missionaries, we have a heart for evangelization and a heart for the fulfillment of the Great Commission. And this wasn't as radical as it may seem. There was a significant, worldwide ecumenical movement of people who felt an urgency to fast and pray for revival in light of the upcoming Jubilee Year of the second millennium. The Church universal was preparing for the year 2000. The three years leading up to the Jubilee were dedicated to each of the three Persons of the Trinity: the Father in 1997, the Holy Spirit in 1998, and the Son in 1999. There was a huge sense of anticipation for what St. John Paul II called a copious amount of grace that would come upon the Church from the Jubilee Year.[12] André and I desired this grace for the spread of the Gospel and the conversion of sinners.

And so we did our research diligently and embarked on this journey Ash Wednesday 1998. The trickiest part of the whole experience was that we had three children to feed. Yep, temptations galore!

---

12 John Paul II, *Incarnationis Mysterium*, 2000, http://www.vatican.va/jubilee_2000/docs/documents/hf_jp-ii_doc_30111998_bolla-jubilee_en.html.

In the final week of the fast, André left for a few days of round-table meetings with Renewal Ministries. I stayed at home with the kids. It was the worst of times; it was the best of times.

I was completely exhausted: physically, mentally, emotionally, and most of all spiritually. It took all my energy to feed and take care of the children. I couldn't wait for nap times and bedtime so I could collapse, cry, and fall asleep.

One day I called a friend of the family and asked if he would take the kids to the pool for the afternoon so I could have respite. After the older two were picked up, I tucked our youngest in for his long afternoon nap and went to my room. I collapsed on the bed, raw and weary. There was nothing left in me—no fervor, no strength, nothing. I was completely spent and exhausted in every way.

My perceived impressive resume of spiritual accomplishments was of no help now. Big deal! None of it could bring me consolation or strength. In fact all I could see was how horribly I had braved the forty-day fast! All I could see were my bad attitudes, temptations, rationalizations, and lack of courage. I was a failure at fasting.

I cried to God for help, slumping to the floor on my knees at the foot of the bed. In this troubled state of prayer, a scene emerged in my mind which depicted what was happening in my soul. I saw myself desperately clutching the feet of the crucified Christ. All around me was darkness, storm, and torrential winds. At its climax the wind was so strong that it lifted me so I was parallel to the ground, but I still desperately clung to the feet of Jesus with all my might, screaming into the wind, "Help me! Jesus! I need you!"

I was in touch with my weakness, my nothingness, and my need for Jesus—my need for a Saviour. Without him I was doomed. And then, a "ding ding ding" went off in my head. *This* was the answer to my prayer. This is really what I had asked God for in 1996—to know, on a visceral level, that I needed Jesus to die on the cross to save me.

Even though I was still just as raw and exhausted, suddenly my tears were no longer rooted in desperation, but in amazement. He had answered my prayer; I knew I needed him. How amazing to know I was so helpless. As we hear in the Easter Vigil Exsultet, "Oh happy fault that won for us so great a Saviour!"

It wasn't just the rawness and weakness brought on by the fast that showed me my need for a Saviour. It was the pinnacle of my two-year journey of giving God permission to invade my privacy—a full two years of humbling realizations, prayers, forgiveness, repentance, and purging.

God's purpose for our lives is more than purging; it's restoration and renovation. The bridegroom and bride imagery so often found in Scripture reveals to us the ultimate end for which we are being fashioned and prepared.

As I was taking in everything that had just happened in that prayer time and was moving into more peaceful sobs and sniffles, a ridiculous thought kept coming into my head. I tried to dismiss it, but to no avail. I kept thinking I should put on my wedding gown. *What? No! I'm not doing that—that's crazy. Not now, not after this prayer experience! Why am I thinking such a thing?*

The more I tried to turn my thoughts to "holy things," the more the idea of putting on my wedding dress persisted. Finally, to appease the Lord, since I knew that it must be his insistent voice, I reached up to the highest shelf of the closet and retrieved my wedding gown. Feeling foolish, and so afraid someone would ring the doorbell at this most inopportune time, I sheepishly and quickly put it on. To my surprise, after losing weight during the forty-day fast, it fit me like a glove.

And so there I was. I sat on the floor in a puddle of taffeta and chiffon, looking at myself in the floor-length mirror, and wondering, "What am I supposed to do now?"

I felt at peace, and I sensed that the Lord was inviting me to sit in this place of calm and stillness. So I sat. I gazed upon my reflection in the mirror. The Lord wanted to give me a taste of my destiny in Christ—to show me that it was his intention to prepare me as his bride.

This major undertaking of restoration, renovation, and reconciliation was undoubtedly the work of God. However, he did not embark on this without my permission and willingness to cooperate with his leading. And he had work in mind for me. He called me to be "engaged," to "trim my lamp" and be ready for his coming, to follow the Bridegroom wherever he would lead. He was restoring me for himself for eternity. He was also restoring my relationships here in this life. Even in the experience of putting on my wedding gown, the Lord was also promising to bring greater love and joy to André and me in our marriage.

The Lord allows us to experience the gritty reality and depths of our weakness in order to restore us. It's an experience of the paschal mystery—Christ's passion, death, and resurrection. It's the path to glory and life eternal.

Questions for Personal Reflection

1. How do I feel about Patti Mansfield's prayer: "Lord, invade my privacy"?

2. How might this prayer help prepare me to be ready to be with the Lord in heaven?

3. What could prevent me from praying a prayer like this?

4. Are there other relationships that come to mind in which I know there is still resentment toward me (or from me toward others)?

—⟐ SEVEN ⟐—
Ongoing Reconciliation

"'How often should I forgive? As many as seven times?' Jesus said to
him, 'Not seven times, but, I tell you, seventy-seven times.'"
—*Matthew 18:21–22*

IT MIGHT HAVE occurred to you that there was no reference to my biological father in the previous chapter. That Lent of extensive repentance did not include dealing with him. First and foremost I was frightened beyond belief of him. I sensed that it wouldn't be a good idea to open up an old, potentially harmful can of worms. However, the fact that I chose not to engage with him didn't mean I hadn't forgiven him. I was still much too afraid, wounded, and fragile for an encounter.

For some people it wouldn't be wise to try to reconcile with someone if that person is dangerous, and such engagement would put them in harm's way. For others it is not possible to engage in reconciliation because the person is inaccessible or deceased.

In my situation, God the Father knew the trembling little girl that I was, who was all but paralyzed with fear of her earthly father, whom I perceived was pure evil. God knew my heart and was protecting and healing it. However, another reason I didn't attempt to reconcile with him was much more practical. He was off the grid; no one knew where he was. He had changed his name, had alienated himself from his only other living relative (his father), and had not been in contact with me since I was twelve.

But I was at peace, and my heart was definitely healing. The Lord in his goodness knows what I can handle.

An Unexpected Invitation

In early summer 1998, I received a random phone call one day from my uncle. None of my ten uncles had *ever* called me! What could be going on? Did someone die? Well, yes actually. My uncle explained to me that my paternal grandfather had died, and that my biological father had contacted him in the hopes of getting a hold of me in regard to the will. He gave me my father's phone number and said I should call him back.

I hung up the phone in a state of shock. *I'm supposed to call him? He wants to talk to me? I'm just supposed to pick up the phone and call him after all I've been through and after all these years! Are you kidding me?*

It had been twenty-five years since I had seen or spoken to him. It's impossible to express how frightening these words were: "He wants you to give him a call." Phoning him was even more terrifying because of a nightmare I had when I was nine years old. In this dream I was trapped in a phone conversation with my father. I was unable to get the phone away from my ear. I was locked into the conversation and couldn't escape it. His voice was twisted, with a terribly sinister and hissing kind of tone. This nightmare came out of the fact that he used to send me messages recorded on cassette. I greatly resented having to listen to them. No one forced me to listen to them, but I somehow felt compelled to. The sound of his voice welled up deep emotions which I surely couldn't identify at such a young age, other than as disgust and terror.

Imagine my horror then, of not only talking to him on the phone but willingly taking the initiative to do so! I sat there on the edge of my bed, stunned, numb, and gripped with fear. I couldn't accept it—it was as though I was in shock or denial. It took me several days before I was able to tell André about it. Every time I thought about telling him what had happened, I choked up. Somehow verbalizing it to another human being would make it real. And then what would I do?

Finally telling André was one thing, but the challenge of actually making the phone call called for an entirely different level of courage and abandonment to God.

It reminded me of the time I went cliff jumping when visiting my friends' cottage. The ledge was at a pretty challenging height, and it seemed even higher when standing on it looking down than surveying it from the water's edge. It can be paralyzing. I found myself frozen on that ledge, trying to psych myself up to jump.

Breathe. Breathe. Breathe. "Okay.... Now! No, no, no, no, wait! Hang on! I'm not ready yet." Breathe. Breathe. Breathe. "Look, you can do this. You're just going to jump. It's simple. All you do is jump. Okay? Let's do it. Ready? Here we go, one, two...wait, wait, wait..."

This self-talk went on for what seemed to be a long time, although it was probably only five minutes. I would have turned around if I could have, but there really was no going back. The path to the jumping ledge was fine coming toward it, but it would have ended in catastrophe leaving by it. The less daunting of the two options was to jump. Breathe. Breathe.

I was standing on a similarly rocky metaphorical cliff that summer Saturday afternoon in our bedroom. Breathe, breathe. The cordless phone was in one hand, the contact information in the other. Breathe. Breathe. "Oh God, help me!" Jump!

It was a leap of faith of mammoth proportion.

I dialed those ten numbers, and I managed to let the phone ring without hanging up. I remember thinking, *Please, please, please don't answer the phone! Please, please go to voicemail...*

"Hello?" said a male voice.

From the moment I replied, "Hello...this is Angèle," I was flooded with an interior lightness, peace, and confidence. It was unmistakably the grace of God—he was lifting me up and making up for my littleness and weakness. The conversation went incredibly well, and to my surprise we were even able to laugh together! It was incredible; it was a miracle. Once again I was experiencing the truth of this verse: "My grace is sufficient for you, for power is made perfect in weakness" (2 Corinthians 12:9). This was another opportunity to choose forgiveness, to choose to release, and to choose to extend loving mercy to a person who had hurt me in a very damaging way.

It's been almost twenty years since that phone call. To be honest I still struggle with how to have an ongoing relationship with my biological father. It's still uncomfortable for a variety of reasons. Regardless of how it feels, though, I continue, with the help of God, to embrace a disposition of mercy.

Living Forgiveness

How do we consistently live out of a place of forgiveness after the initial experience of forgiving? It continues to boil down to what Fr. Lauer says: forgiveness is a choice, not a feeling. We need to remember this and anchor ourselves in this truth, because we will face a myriad of temptations in this area. We might wonder, *How do I know I've forgiven this person when I'm still struggling with so much frustration?*

The frustration might come from struggling with painful memories; it could come from having to deal with the person we've forgiven who is still doing the same old stuff, providing us with new reasons to prove we shouldn't have to be merciful after all.

The Situation Seems Harder Than Before

From experience I can tell you that the enemy wanted me to doubt that I forgave fervently enough for it to be efficacious. "If you really forgave him, you wouldn't feel so angry still," that negative voice said inside my head. By the virtue of the fact that I was now more aware of my wounds and resentments, I noticed them more than I had before. This was confusing. It seemed as if things were actually worse than before I chose to forgive. They weren't worse, though; I was just so much more aware of my interior motives. It felt as if I was reacting with less charity than I had before I chose to forgive, but that also was not true. The truth was I was no longer oblivious to my behaviours. I learned that it's really important not to get discouraged in this phase of living out forgiveness. It might look worse, but in reality I was simply more aware.

Forgiveness doesn't automatically result in "forget mode" in our brains. We might continue to remember it all. In these situations we have an opportunity to reassert the forgiveness we've already done. I've had to say to myself and God, "These feelings are coming up again, very strongly in fact, and I'm not going to go there. I've already chosen to forgive and release this person. I stand by that decision. This has already been dealt with, and I'm not changing my mind. I choose forgiveness again. I choose life."

This is another example of the benefit of verbally admitting our failures (and forgiveness) to another human being. Because it was so concretely done and witnessed by someone else, we can be reminded that we actually did release these issues and people. It really happened!

I have had to talk back to Satan and put my foot down on occasion. "No, this has been dealt with, released, and placed at the foot of the cross of Jesus Christ. By his cross and resurrection he has redeemed the world, and given us his mercy. I do not own this problem any longer, and you do not have authority here, either. Jesus is the Master and King of this entire situation. I submit it to him, I trust in him, and I will listen to his voice alone. You must flee!"

Such intensity is necessary at times. You need to stand against the enemy in the authority of the name of Jesus and your dignity as a child of the Father. As St. James said, "Resist the devil and he will flee" (James 4:7).

You can also invite the Holy Spirit to reveal any remaining root of unforgiveness that you need to deal with. Perhaps there are some "dandelions" you missed. Or perhaps you failed to remove a "splinter in the wound" that is now festering and must come out. Search your heart and ask the Lord if there is anything else you need to deal with. Talk to your priest or spiritual director about it. If there's something to deal with, deal with it. If not, then choose again to stand by your original decision to forgive, repent, and release.

The Person Still Treats Me the Same Way

Sometimes a person we've forgiven still engages in the same kind of behaviours that have hurt us in the past. In these situations I've prayed something like this: "Lord, I forgive her again. You ask me to forgive seventy times seven times, and so, Lord, I will. I release her to your justice again. Forgive me for judging her for 'always' doing things to me. Give me the grace to forgive again."

As you can see, the choice to forgive begins with a big first step, but it involves many resolutions to confirm that decision. As Martin Luther King Jr. said, "Forgiveness is not an occasional act, it is a constant attitude."[13]

When you're healing a forgiveness wound, it will be tender for a while, just as a flesh wound would be. Physical wounds form a scab as they heal. The scab gets itchy and uncomfortable, and we are very aware of it. We are tempted to pick at the scab, but as we all know, when we keep picking at scabs, they don't heal. (When our oldest daughter was two years old, she had a mosquito bite on her forehead that she kept picking at. It lasted from summer all the way to Christmas! I have photos to prove it.)

Time heals all wounds, as the saying goes. We need to be patient with ourselves, as we are with physical healing. We must choose not to reopen old wounds, but rather to let them heal. Over time, and with God's grace, the pain of the memories won't sting as harshly.

Lessons from St. Maria Goretti

When I question myself as to whether I've forgiven or not, I find the life of St. Maria Goretti teaches powerful and practical lessons.

Maria Goretti was an eleven-year-girl who was cornered by a young man, Alessandro Serenelli. She refused to submit to his sexual advances. In his rage at her resistance, he attacked her with a knife and stabbed her fourteen times. At the hospital, before she died, the priest who came to give her the last rites asked her if she had forgiven Alessandro. She replied, "Yes, I forgive him and want him to be in paradise with me someday."

To me this is the secret to identifying whether I have a forgiving disposition or not: "Do I desire and hope that one who has offended me will be in heaven someday?"

I've heard this explained another way by some holy Sisters of the Presentation of Mary. They taught me to ask myself, "Do I sincerely desire good and blessing for this person's life?"

---

13 http://aboutmartinlutherking.com/45/2013/05/15/forgiveness-is-not-an-occasional-act-it-is-a-constant-attitude-martin-luther-king-jr/.

These are helpful questions for self-examination. What I like about them is that they still provide a certain amount of freedom in terms of how I am to engage with the other person here and now. Although we are asked by God to forgive everyone and love everyone—even our enemies—it doesn't mean we have to stick around and get abused by them. Sometimes the person or the relationship is not healthy, and there is need for distance and protection.

Romans 12:18 provides a key: "If it is possible, so far as it depends on you, live peaceably with all." That "if" is pretty important. "*If* it is possible..."—in some situations it is *not* possible to live peaceably with someone. The advice and discernment of trusted friends, a spiritual director, or counsellor can help us to navigate these sensitive situations.

On occasion, a "time out" from a particular relationship allowed my own healing to happen while the other person grew in maturity. Sometimes I've been advised by my spiritual director or a close friend not to engage in a relationship with someone for my own safety. And in countless moments, I have remained at or returned to a place where I had to make the choice for forgiveness. I have had to put my foot down and say to myself and God, "I choose mercy. I choose to desire this person's good, his or her blessing, and his or her welcome into heaven."

Incidentally, there's more to the story of St. Maria Goretti and Alessandro Serenelli.

Alessandro was sentenced to thirty years in prison for his crime of passion against Maria. During his eighth year in prison, an incredible thing happened. Maria appeared to him in a vivid dream, offering him fourteen lilies, representing the number of stab wounds he had inflicted on her. The experience led to his complete conversion. After fulfilling his jail sentence, he sought out Maria's mother to ask for her forgiveness. Her response to him was to lovingly place her hands on his face and say, "Alessandro, Marietta [Maria] forgave you, Christ has forgiven you, and why should I not also forgive. I forgive you, my son!"[14]

---

14 Assunta Goretti, quoted in James Likoudia, "St. Maria Goretti and Her Murderer," MariaGoretti.org, http://www.mariagoretti.org/likoudisarticle2.htm.

The next day Maria's mother and Alessandro went to Mass at the village's parish together. After Mass Alessandro repented publically for what he had done. What a witness! Although he had made peace with the Church in the sacrament of reconciliation, he went further and sought to be reconciled directly with the people and the community his sins had affected.

On June 24, 1950, fifty years after her death, little Maria Goretti was canonized. Both mother and murderer would sit side by side in St. Peter's Square to witness it. They had made peace with each other and with their God.

St. Maria Goretti, pray for us!

Alessandro went on to live the rest of his days as a tertiary of the Franciscans, serving as a gardener for one of the communities. His conversion is an incredible story. Maria's mother, Assunta, was also amazing. Her generosity, charity, mercy, and kindness toward Alessandro is beyond comprehension. It is not natural. It is supernatural—and beautiful.

Forgiving the Unrepentant

It is a particular quandary when we know we are called to forgive someone, but they are unrepentant. Perhaps they are simply oblivious that they have hurt us. That's a bit easier to deal with. But what about people who don't believe they have done anything hurtful? What if they dismiss our feelings, claiming that we're overreacting? What if they are just mean-spirited and don't care that they have offended us? What if what they did to us was unbelievably terrible and they don't care (betrayal, rape, abuse)? Do we still need to forgive? These situations are a real cross to bear.

As Catholics we say things like, "This is a cross to bear" pretty often as a way to describe a tough situation which requires faith and courage. But forgiving an unrepentant, spiteful person who has hurt us is a *real* cross—it actually is being in communion with the cross of Christ. "Father, forgive them; for they do not know what they are doing" (Luke 23:34).

Jesus's goodness, miracles, love, and preaching were completely misunderstood by his enemies; everything Jesus did enflamed them to seek to silence him and stop him. Out of love of us, he allowed them to capture him and submitted himself to their vengeance. Even from the humiliation and excruciating pain of the cross, he spoke of forgiveness. His intention and commitment to mercy was not just for the generic "us," but it was also for "them"—a gaggle of unrepentant, mocking murderers.

When we are the ones challenged to forgive someone who is not repentant, we must fix our eyes on Jesus, "the pioneer and perfecter of our faith, who for the sake of the joy that was set before him endured the cross, disregarding its shame, and has taken his seat at the right hand of the throne of God. Consider him who endured such hostility against himself from sinners, so that you may not grow weary or lose heart" (Hebrews 12:2–3).

We might be tempted, because of a person's belligerence, to feel we are justified to stay in a place of unforgiveness. We cannot give in to this! This would be a grave mistake. We must choose to release and forgive this person. If we can't extend our own mercy, we can at least focus on being conduits of Jesus's divine mercy. "I will unite my will with the mercy of Jesus. I choose to forgive with Christ and like him."

We can also imitate people like St. Maria Goretti, Assunta Goretti, or the family of Ardeth Wood. There are many witnesses to supernatural forgiveness. One example is Pastor Dale Lang of Taber, Alberta, whose son Jason was murdered in a school shooting. On the nationally televised funeral service, Pastor Dale spoke of his forgiveness for the young man who had killed his son:

> *Dom Lorenzo Scupoli in* The Spiritual Combat *tells us, "Nothing can be more noble or approach the divine nature more closely than to forgive those who injure us and to return good for evil." The love Jesus had forgave and released those who mocked and killed him. I am commanded to love as he loved. It's clear what he is asking of me. I am to forgive always, everyone without exception, even those whom I might perceive to be an enemy to my happiness. We are companions with Christ when we extend mercy and seek to imitate him who loved us at our worst.*

Cinderella...Again

I hope you're not rolling your eyes at another mention of Cinderella, but I just have to talk about her again. Disney's recent live-action adaptation (released in 2015) was not only delightful and magical; it also demonstrated how to live a life characterized by mercy.

When Cinderella is at her mother's deathbed, her mother tenderly holds her hand and speaks words of affirmation. "Cinderella, you have more kindness in your little finger than most people do in their whole lifetime." She then exhorts Cinderella—who incidentally is about the same age as St. Maria Goretti—to promise her that she will always live out of the strength of her kindness. "Promise me. Remember. Kindness and Courage."

Cinderella solemnly and sincerely replies, "I promise."

Kindness and Courage. These two words will take us far in life as we strive to live out forgiveness, mercy, and reconciliation. Often situations come to mind when I think, *If I could have practiced kindness and courage, I'm pretty sure things would have turned out much differently!* I am, unfortunately, lacking in both kindness and courage. I am quite talented, however, at grumpy and wimpy!

In my relationships I easily get focused on how I feel I'm being treated. "He's being pretty snarky toward me." "She's totally judging my outfit." I inadvertently give off vibes that mirror my perception.. I might act defensively or aggressively to protect myself. All of this is ultimately concerned with how I am being treated. The word *kindness* acts as a compass orienting me to treat each person with dignity, respect, and charity.

Charity is a classic Catholic word epitomizing virtue, but I find the word *kindness* to be less intimidating. Maybe it's because kindness is new to me, or because Cinderella said it, but kindness helps me to grasp how to act with charity. I see charity as something very holy people do, people like Mother Teresa. Charity comes across as self-sacrificing, generous, and heroic—all qualities I'm not very good at exhibiting. If I wore a blue-and-white habit of the Sisters of Charity (Mother Teresa's order), maybe I could pull off some convincing charity, but that's doubtful at best. Charity is impressive, and I'm just not that impressive.

But I actually might be able to wrap my mind around kindness! I certainly could attempt kindness much better than charity. Yes, I'll go with kindness.

I know that I personally like being treated with kindness. It's nice; kindness dissolves the crusty and grumpy experiences and people we encounter. Nothing gets me more worked up than dealing with crusty and grumpy customer-service agents, be it at the airport, a hotel, an insurance company, or a utility company. I react to their tone instantly, although I'm sure they are reacting to all the stress I'm dealing with, let alone the fifty people they dealt with prior to me. I can hear the disdain and sarcasm in their tone of voice, and I immediately think, *They're not going to help me out. They're not listening. They don't give a rip about me. This stinks.* Consequently my tone escalates, and when the flurry of frustration ends, I look back at it and realize I definitely could have handled that better.

But what if I could have offered my responses to "Mrs. CrankyPants" there from a disposition of kindness? I might not be able to imagine myself "practicing charity" in these kinds of tense situations, but I might be able to imagine God helping me to act with kindness.

Kindness works. Kindness can diffuse the tension and can even give Mrs. CrankyPants the freedom to change her tone, too. Kindness shown to others, even to those who are most difficult to love, is an occasion to apply charity and forgiveness in a practical way.

Cinderella's mother encourages her to respond with kindness and courage. Courage ensures that kindness is not weakness. Courage with kindness is another way of expressing what St. Paul says, "Speak the truth in love" (see Ephesians 4:15). Kindness respects the dignity of the other person; courage respects our own dignity.

In the film we see Cinderella's integrity and commitment to honour her mother's request. In all her dealings with her stepmother and stepsisters, she keeps her poise and acts with kindness. She has every reason to do the opposite and act out in vengeance and anger. But to honour her parents' memory and out of affection for them, she does the right thing. She can be courageous because she knows the value and dignity she enjoys as their beloved daughter.

My courage is ultimately rooted in the conviction that I am a beloved daughter of God. I am loved, secure, protected, and have great personal value. I have nothing to be afraid of. Nothing can separate me from my Father's love.

I have courage because I am firm in *who* I am and *whose* I am. I know what I mean to the great I AM. I am his, and he is mine. Possessing courage rooted in this filial relationship with Almighty God, I should be able to speak to anyone—even my enemy—with kindness. Courage says, "I will not be afraid of you or your words, because I know my value. I know the One who created me, and he has a high purpose in mind for me. I am not afraid that, if I choose to treat you kindly, in spite of how you have mistreated me, I will lose out or be taken advantage of."

I refuse to believe that my kindness will negate God's justice and goodness toward me. Since I know I am a beloved daughter of God, I choose to act according to the dignity, maturity, poise, and kindness characteristic of a child of the Most High God.

Courage for me—kindness for you. Courage to root me in my dignity—kindness to treat you with dignity. Courage, rooted in the Father's love, is how I will carry myself, as I treat you with kindness, a fruit of the Holy Spirit's transformative work in me.

As God's chosen ones, holy and beloved, clothe yourselves with compassion, kindness, humility, meekness, and patience. Bear with one another and, if anyone has a complaint against another, forgive each other; just as the Lord has forgiven you, so you also must forgive. Above all, clothe yourselves with love, which binds everything together in perfect harmony. And let the peace of Christ rule in your hearts, to which indeed you were called in the one body. And be thankful. Let the word of Christ dwell in you richly; teach and admonish one another in all wisdom; and with gratitude in your hearts sing psalms, hymns, and spiritual songs to God. And whatever you do, in word or deed, do everything in the name of the Lord Jesus, giving thanks to God the Father through him. (Colossians 3:12–17)

I'm proposing a Cinderella-inspired type of examen for practicing mercy in your interpersonal relationships. (I hope St. Ignatius won't mind the adaptation.) The examen is a tool for reviewing your day to see how you have responded (or not responded) to God's action in your life.

What I'm proposing here is an examen rooted in the conviction of your identity as a child of God, the assurance of the Holy Spirit's power to help you act with courage and kindness, and the confidence that you are extending the same mercy to others that Christ has given you.

First, before, or even as an interaction is unfolding initially, turn inwardly and invoke the Holy Spirit's presence.

Holy Spirit, I welcome you here in this situation. I give you permission. Father God, thank you for assuring me that I am your beloved child. You care for me. You are my rock and my fortress.

Second, with the Holy Spirit's help, choose to honour God and act with kindness and courage.

I choose to live out of my dignity as a child of God and act now with courage and kindness toward (person's name). Jesus, in light of your kindness and love toward me, I will honour you and act likewise now. Help me Lord! Kindness and courage! Amen.

There and Back Again

Let's return to the beginning of this chapter where I shared the story of my reconciliation with my biological father. It was a colossal step toward peace and healing for both of us. And considering my deep-seated fears, I can't help but think of the encounter in terms of another movie: *Star Wars.*[15]

Darth Vader, the man in the black helmet and cape with the heavy breathing issues, is the instrument of the Dark Side of

---

15 *Star Wars Episode VI,* dir. by George Lucas (Los Angeles: Twentieth Century Fox, 1983).

the Force seeking to overthrow and control the Republic. Luke Skywalker heroically seeks to defeat Darth Vader and then discovers the horrifying truth that Darth Vader is his father.

I remember raptly watching this scene when it first came out in the early 1980s and thinking, *Oh my gosh, Luke! My real father is an evil monster, too!* (Keep in mind that I was only thirteen years old—everything is dramatic when you're thirteen.)

After the reconciliation with my biological father, what particularly struck me was the intimate redemption scene just before Darth Vader's death in Episode VI: *Return of the Jedi*. Vader asks Luke to remove his mask so he can see Luke with his own eyes before he dies.

As Luke removes the mask of the monster, we finally see Anakin Skywalker in the flesh. He is weak, pitiable, and vulnerable. His appearance is grotesque, but his eyes capture your attention. They are soft as they behold the face of his only son. His unveiled eyes reveal the deepest emotions of his heart: regret, the longing for peace, and the desire to love and be loved.

The encounter with my biological father was a very similar unveiling. He was not the monster of my childhood imaginings. He was simply a man who was hurting and needed compassion.

There is much more to this relationship than I am prepared to share in this book, but suffice it to say that it doesn't have a TV ending, which wraps up problems neatly in the span of half an hour. For healthy personal reasons André and I, along with my spiritual director, have discerned appropriate boundaries. I pray for my father, send cards and gifts on birthdays and Christmas, and generally keep in touch with him. What inspires my actions, as simple as they are, is the same disposition as St. Maria Goretti's. I desire for him to be in heaven, and I hope I will be with him there someday.

St. Maria Goretti, Cinderella, and Luke Skywalker, each in their own way, remind me to fight for forgiveness and reconciliation in relationships. In my humble opinion, they embody Romans 12:21, a verse which has given me perspective on many occasions. "Do not be overcome by evil, but overcome evil with good."

Questions for Personal Reflection

1. How have I experienced the Lord strengthening me to reconcile with someone I felt too weak to deal with?

2. *Have I ever made a decision to forgive that involved a battle with my own emotions? How did I (or could I) turn to God for help with that?*

3. *Have things ever seemed worse in my relationship with someone after trying to forgive him or her? What might give me perspective when faced with that kind of situation again?*

4. *What might I do when a person I have forgiven for a certain behaviour continues to act in the same way?*

5. *Do I struggle with doubts, wondering if I've really forgiven certain people in my life?*

6. *Considering the people I have forgiven, can I say about each of them that I desire and hope they will be with me in heaven someday?*

7. *How might an orientation of kindness and courage have changed some of the interactions I've had in the past?*

—⟨∅⟩ EIGHT ⟨∅⟩—

Forgiveness and the Family

"He will turn the hearts of parents to their children and the hearts of children to their parents."
—*Malachi 4:6*

THERE IS NO shortage of opportunities to practice forgiveness, repentance, and reconciliation, especially in one's family. The opportunities present themselves like magic.

It's kind of like housework. Even after doing full-blown renovations and making your house look amazing, stylish, and efficient, it won't stay in "staged" perfection. If you plan on actually residing in your newly renovated home, you should beware that your lived presence will cause dirty floors, bathrooms, and counters. Your home will accumulate garbage, fingerprints, and smelly laundry. It's startling how quickly my family can sabotage my perfectly cleaned house. (Yes, there are nine of us living in one house, but still it would be nice to make it to the next morning still living in a "show home.")

Showing mercy is a lot like living in our homes. Mercy is where we truly live, and it requires constant care and cleanup. Cleaning up relationships involves forgiving and asking for forgiveness. It's as much a life skill to master and teach your children as doing laundry, washing floors, and scrubbing toilets. We've made it a priority to give our children the skills to know how to give and receive mercy. Although it's important for the well-being of our family, we want to instill these habits so our children can be formed spiritually and go on to live healthy adult lives. We teach our kids how to do household chores so they can be self-sustaining adults, don't we? Learning how to say "I'm sorry" and "I forgive you" will take our children much farther than learning how to iron. (I still don't know how to iron.)

Our child who struggled so much with saying "sorry" that he could only write "S" on a piece of paper now is our best "repenter." It's not unusual for him to come to our bedroom at 11:00 p.m. and say, "Sorry for how I talked to you today." To which we reply, "We forgive you. Thank you for saying 'sorry.'"

A principle we've taught our children is never going to bed angry. As the Bible says, "Be angry but do not sin; do not let the sun go down on your anger" (Ephesians 4:26).

We've also taught our children to be specific. Instead of rattling off a long list of excuses to rationalize what has been done, just name the offense. (For the record, there's nothing wrong with explaining why you acted the way you acted, but ultimately it's about admitting what you did that was hurtful.)

The final principle is acknowledging the person who has just repented, forgiving him or her and affirming the person for apologizing.

By the way, when teaching these principles to our children we've had a particular approach that you might not expect. For example, with the whole "S" situation, we accepted the "S" and all it stood for. We did not berate this child or require him to say a complete sentence apology with precisely the right tone of regret in his voice. We knew it was too much to ask this strong-willed child to do at this point in his maturity. The "S" spoke volumes.

Our mercy toward him spoke volumes, too. This child knew the kind of apology we were specifically looking for. He also knew that our acceptance of the written "S" was a gesture of mercy and kindness; he knew we understood his struggle with pride and stubbornness. We used subsequent situations—and believe me, they were plentiful and abundant—to encourage him to say "sorry" more fully and properly.

When we taught out kids to reply "I forgive you" to the one who just apologized, we gave them some leeway. It's really hard to say "I forgive you" for someone who is still reeling from the pain of what just happened. To force the one who has been hurt to say "I forgive you" on demand is not fair, and it diminishes his or her right to choose to forgive.

We also taught our children that when the one seeking peace says "sorry," it is very hard if the apology is not received and acknowledged. It leaves the one who just apologized feeling vulnerable. We taught them that if someone has humbled himself to apologize, it's important to respond. The approach we instilled in our kids to acknowledge the one repenting even when the wronged party was still upset was to say something like, "Yes, I forgive you, but I'm still really (mad/angry/sad/hurt) right now. I will get over it, but right now I need some space." In this way the one repenting isn't left hanging, and the one who has been hurt hasn't been forced to suppress his or her pain and "get over it" just because the other person apologized.

I think it's okay for the one who did the hurting to see that there are repercussions from what he or she did. "Wow, I really hurt her. She's still really upset even though I said 'sorry.'" This is a good opportunity to teach the kids about penance. I would say, "You can see that your sister is really angry and hurt about what you did. What could you do to prove to her that you're sorry and that you want to make up for what you did?" Sometimes the child would come up with something like a special treat, or playing with something the child doesn't normally share, or offering to do the other sibling's chores. These gestures of sincerity were well received by the one who was hurt, but I think the lesson they taught the offender about penance, empathy, and reconciliation was invaluable.

Reconciliation with Adult Members of the Family

Daily, if not hourly, there are many opportunities to practice forgiveness, mercy, and reconciliation in family life, and the opportunities do not diminish with age. Many people I've spoken with over the years have shared painful stories of severed or damaged relationships in their families. It might be adult siblings who won't come to the same family gatherings, a daughter who rejects her parents' authority in her life with self-destructive behaviour, a son whose anger is a ticking time bomb, a father who is disengaged and avoids the family by investing time and money in addictive behaviours, or a mother, embittered by life, who constantly spews negativity and criticism.

A particular source of pain for Christians is other family members rejecting or attacking them for their faith. It is certainly difficult to have loved ones reject that which you love most, especially when they are rejecting God and blaming you for it.

Jennifer had her conversion when her children were fairly young. She was transformed as she experienced the joy of being loved by God. She was involved in mom faith-sharing groups in her neighborhood and loved the fellowship she was experiencing. Her husband was fine with the fact that she had found a new thing to keep her happy and occupied, but he let her know that his involvement in the Church would be limited to Sunday attendance. She became very active in her faith, attending various events, retreats, and conferences. Her spiritual maturity needed a great deal of work, and her progress was fairly slow. She was frankly more interested in being fed, having fellowship, and getting attention than in real interior transformation. Her neediness caused her to be quite self-focused and rather negligent in her parenting skills. She was more committed to her church activities than she was to caring for her home and her two boys.

By the time her boys got to high school, they wanted nothing to do with church. They resented her preaching at them and generally disrespected her. They felt she was more interested and excited about religion than she was about them. They couldn't stand how phony and nice she acted around church people, while at home she was weak, angry, and yelled all the time. In her anxiousness to win them back, Jennifer became all the more needy, clingy, and preachy.

Jennifer has come to realize she made mistakes in how she raised her boys. She knows she didn't invest in them. She was too caught up in getting attention and feeling inspired at her church events. She regrets what she has done, but she can't turn back time. She wants to win her boys back. She wants to bring them to faith. She dreams of the day they will all go to church together again, like they used to when the boys were in elementary school.

Stories like these are plentiful and painful. Reconciliation is jeopardized because repentance will not be accepted, and forgiveness will not be given.

One of Jennifer's adult sons came to her house one night to borrow some tools. He conveniently stopped by just before supper and let his mother twist his arm to stay for a home-cooked meal. Jennifer wanted so badly for everything to go well, and at first it seemed to be. The conversation was pleasant as Brian and his dad discussed the project he needed the tools for. The meal was a hit, and Jennifer even happened to have dessert. Her husband left shortly after supper for a course he was taking. Jennifer finally had a chance to go a little deeper; she was anxious for healing and restoration.

"Brian, how are you doing, honey?"

"I'm happy, Mom; things are good."

"That makes me so happy. You know I want so much for you." Tears started to well in her eyes, and her voice got that little tremor.

Brian shifted in his seat, muttering under his breath, "Oh man, Mom. Don't start with this again."

"Brian, I am going away on a retreat this weekend, and I would be so happy if you could find it in your heart to forgive me for anything I've done to hurt you."

What happened next was definitely not how the scene had been playing out in Jennifer's mind—where he would hug her and say, "Of course I forgive you, Mom, and I'm so sorry for being a jerk to you."

What actually happened was a flurry of abrupt sounds. The screech of a chair pushing back, the jangle of keys, the slamming of doors, and some colourful language. "Just keep your religion out of my face! I've got to go." Ouch.

What kind of advice and consolation can we give the "Jennifers" of the world?

Truth and Specifics

I would start with the basics, emphasising the need for a thorough examination in order to repent well—in the sacrament of confession and to the person(s) who have been hurt. Remember the twelve-step advice to admit the exact nature of our failures to another human being. This applies to the sacrament of reconciliation, but also to the interaction necessary with the one offended.

Notice that Jennifer basically said to Brian, "I am so sorry if there's anything I might have done that may have hurt you." In my opinion this has got to be the laziest and most pathetic repentance possible. "If there's anything I might have done that may have hurt you…" This mastery of evasiveness says nothing specific, shows minimal ownership of wrong, and practically faults the person for being overly sensitive and offended. We need to tell a person we've hurt exactly what we did. We need to say it truthfully and properly. In the words of Jesus, "the truth will set you free" (John 8:32). This is the beauty of the sacrament of reconciliation when we tell a priest in the confessional precisely what we have done.

After conferring with Dr. Mary Healy about this, a word of caution: I suggest that you get advice from your priest or spiritual director about the value of revealing what you have done to an innocent or oblivious person—for example, telling a child you had an adulterous encounter. In these situations we must discern whether "honesty is the best policy." The expression, as Dr. Healy describes it,

> *implies that if one is truly honest, one will disclose an adulterous affair to one's children. But this confuses honesty with disclosure. Being perfectly honest does not mean one must tell everything to everyone; and conversely, to not disclose something does not mean you are being a little bit dishonest. The appropriateness of disclosing something like this depends on a whole variety of circumstances. I think there are many cases where it would be inappropriate and hurtful to do so.*

Our concern should be for the person receiving the news. Ultimately our disposition is obeying the Lord's promptings and being willing to do whatever he asks of us for healing and reconciliation to happen.

Thank goodness for holy friends who can coach us and help us discern the Lord's voice.

As you work on those "Jennifer and Brian" types of relationships, my advice is to continue to strive to have a loving, forgiving disposition. In your heart pray and release them to God. Pray that the Holy Spirit will help them to be open to reconciliation. Pray for the relationship to be protected from the attacks of the enemy, who only desires "to steal, kill, and destroy" (John 10:10).

You might also want to try subtle ways to reach out and be kind, to let these individuals know you have left the door to the relationship open from your end. Perhaps let them know when the next big family event is happening and emphasise that they are most welcome to join the gang. Perhaps you could pop a simple but meaningful gift on someone's front porch that could speak volumes and help thaw the icy landscape. It might be as simple as a vintage board game you spied at a garage sale which is loaded with memories and inside jokes.

When Jennifer's relationship with her boys started slipping out of her hands, she tried harder to recover them through smothering them or nagging them for attention. A more effective way to deal with the situation would be to release them, entrusting her sons, their future, and her relationship with them to God. (And even if she can't perfectly release them, she could try to hold the reins ever so much more lightly!)

Time and Space

Adages such as "time heals all wounds" and "this too shall pass" are helpful to give perspective. I believe softness and openness can return with the passing of time and giving everyone some space (along with your prayers, patience, kindness, and goodness).

A leadership principle espoused by Joseph Grenny is "clicks in the flywheel": the idea that lasting change happens through deliberate, intentional, consistent, persistent effort. If you keep working the plan, the plan will work. Take it one step at a time. It's a tortoise-and-hare sort of approach—slow and steady wins the race. I think this leadership approach applies (in corporate speak) to the growth, development, and change management in relationships. Care, prayer, and kindness consistently and patiently lived through faith in God and docility to his promptings, in his time, will bear fruit.

Trust in the LORD, and do good; so you will live in the land, and enjoy security. Take delight in the LORD, and he will give you the desires of your heart. Commit your way to the LORD; trust in him, and he will act. He will make your vindication shine like the light, and the justice of your cause like the noonday. Be still before the LORD, and wait patiently for him; do not fret over those who prosper in their way, over those who carry out evil devices. Refrain from anger, and forsake wrath. Do not fret—it leads only to evil. (Psalm 37:3–8)

I believe that I shall see the goodness of the LORD in the land of the living. Wait for the LORD; be strong, and let your heart take courage; wait for the LORD! (Psalm 27:13–14)

Even when it seems like all this kindness and patience is pointless and hasn't led to any positive change, we need to keep perspective. Ultimately the "win" is not that those we've offended make their peace with us, but that in the end they will make their peace with God. And if that is what our clicks in the flywheel contribute toward, then a lifetime of struggle and pain will be worth it to spend an eternity of joy with them in heaven.

Growth and Maturity

Another consequence of the passing of time is growth. Time gives people the chance to grow up! People's overreactions and outbursts often come from a lack of maturity. The wounds and circumstances of life affect proper development and maturation. It is a paradigm shift to realize that someone might not have the capacity to react properly because of the effects of his or her woundedness. It's almost as though the person is handicapped. You would have much more patience and modify your expectations for someone who had a heart defect in a race, or for an ESL student in a speech competition. With time and practice these individuals could become fierce competitors—but it will take time for them to mature and develop. This perspective, which I gained from my spiritual director, has helped me to be patient and seek to understand where another person might be coming from and the many challenges he or she may have faced in life.

When faced with immature outbursts, the challenge is not to stoop to that level, but to respond and conduct yourself with maturity, wisdom, and goodness.

It's not easy for me to keep my cool. I get sucked into immaturity way too often. Whenever I get in an argument with a five-year old, I spontaneously want to revert to the fighting tactics of a five-year-old:

"Pick up your crayons."

"I don't want to."

"So what?* Pick them up anyway."

"Why should I?"

You see that asterisk. There. Right there, at that point, three seconds into the conversation, I'm already parenting with the maturity of a five-year-old.

As a parent and as a disciple of Christ, I need to remember to "act my age." When I respond to someone who is younger or more immature or wounded, I should anticipate that the conversation might get messy, and I should prepare myself to handle it with poise and maturity, refraining from imitating the other person's tone and behaviour. As I often coach myself when dealing with an obstinate child (mine or someone else's), "Who's the adult here?"

"Me." Okay, then I need to act like one.

It never helps to calm a person down who is freaking out by freaking out in kind. Instead my self-control can help the person get a grip and regain his or her own composure. It's a bit tricky sometimes, though, not to come across as haughty and condescending as you model the maturity the other person is lacking.

Exercising Empathy

Hurting individuals might not want to talk to you, but if you can get them talking, chances are they are not interested in hearing your assessment of their life. They probably are bracing themselves for your preaching. Preaching isn't a good approach, but empathy is. Empathy is being willing to sit with a person in his or her situation and pain, and appreciate what the person has been dealing with. Empathy is way of living Cinderella's kindness and courage. It's the courage not to be repulsed or afraid of what someone else has experienced while being prepared to acknowledge what is going on. Empathy is the kindness to be gentle and respectful as you listen and learn about a person's life. It is the kindness to refrain from moving on too quickly or dismissing his or her need to share.

Empathy is a beautiful gift. It requires a great deal of maturity to put another person's needs first. When your actions are the subject of the pain being expressed by that person, it's challenging to be empathetic. In this case empathy means really listening to how you have hurt a person and appreciating the pain he or she feels because of you. It takes a gargantuan amount of courage, humility, and maturity to say, "I hear you. I am so sorry. I want you to know you can tell me more. I want to know how you are hurting because of me."

Empathy incorporates active listening—with accompanying affirmative sounds and words. Active listening does not interrupt and is mindful of using appropriate body language such as nodding, leaning forward, and making occasional eye contact.

You might be surprised that I said *occasional* eye contact. Think about it, though. If you are sharing your deepest pain, do you really want someone staring at you the whole time? Wouldn't you find that to be way too intense? I say go with occasional eye contact, because this gives the other person the freedom to look at you and catch your eye without feeling assessed the whole time.

Empathy can't be given to a person who isn't ready to receive it. Sometimes the person pushes us away, along with our offer of empathy. We need to consider the other person's point of view. The past wounds and relationships have eroded his or her trust. How can a person who has received far too little love or care in life be vulnerable with someone else? Maybe the person won't give you a chance to be empathetic because you are perceived as the source of his or her pain.

Mona's Story

My friend Mona was very active in her parish and in various movements in the Church. She asked to meet me for lunch one day and confided that she was sick at heart over trying to reconcile with her cousin and his wife. They were so angry with her and her husband that they all but refused to talk to them. The bulk of the issues that had accumulated were between Mona and her cousin's wife, Pam. Pam had many insecurities growing up, having lost her father at a young age. Her first marriage had failed, and after marrying Mona's cousin Jim, she was completely cared for and served by this protective, generous husband.

Mona, a hardworking and capable woman, was frustrated by how Pam allowed Jim to serve her hand and foot. Sometimes Mona's frustrations were hard to hide, especially at family gatherings when Pam could always be found resting on the couch or taking care of her dog (which she insisted on bringing to family dinners) while Jim, Mona, and others cleaned up after dinner.

One day a relatively small conflict—a disagreement over the next family gathering—was the straw that broke the camel's back. As usual Mona was expected to take the lead, because she always did. The conflict came when Pam suggested that everyone chip in money to hire a chef to cook for the family. It might have been a good idea, except it was twice as expensive as going out to a restaurant. Mona rolled her eyes and sighed. Bob spoke up and said the idea wasn't reasonable for their budget. Pam exploded in tears, yelling specifically at Mona. She pointed her finger at Mona and said, "I'm sick and tired of you not respecting me. I've had it with this family. Until I can be treated properly, I want nothing to do with you!"

Mona and Bob were heartsick. They were a very close-knit family, getting together at least one Sunday a month as well as on all the major holidays. They didn't want this kind of a rift in the family, and they certainly didn't want to be the ones responsible for it. All the more humiliating was that they were the practicing Christians in the family! Even though they had experienced long-standing frustrations with Pam, they tried to set aside their annoyance and ignore her behavior.

Mona shared with me that, after much reflection, she could see how she had disrespected Pam in her heart. She recognized how that attitude came out in the way she treated Pam, and she confessed that she often had talked about her behind her back. Mona had gone to confession and sought out various ways to try to open the dialogue and welcome Jim and Pam back into the life of the family. None of her attempts were welcomed.

Eventually Bob and Jim collaborated to set up a meeting for Mona and Pam to talk. The meeting happened, but it was a disaster. Pam refused to talk, and Mona was intimidated by Pam's silence.

After almost a year of strain and pain, signs of life and reconciliation started to emerge. Time helped—as the weeks and months passed, the edge of the situation began to wear off. Prayer helped immensely during that time of waiting. Mona and Bob grew in humility and docility to the Lord as they examined their hearts and sought his direction and healing for the family.

They exercised empathy with Jim and Pam by "getting" that Pam wasn't ready for reconciliation. Their challenge was to be mature and empathetic by backing off (without recoiling and pouting from the rejection). They kept their composure, prayed for Jim and Pam, and made various attempts to leave the door of the relationship open for when they might be ready to reconnect— even if it was as simple as sending a text to wish one of them a happy birthday.

Bob and Mona's commitment to patience, humility, maturity, and prayer eventually bore the fruit of reconciliation. The two couples finally had a proper talk. Bob and Mona strove to embrace maturity and took the high ground by clearly confessing their failures to Jim and Pam. They practiced empathy by sincerely listening to Pam and Jim tell their point of view, expressing regret for their words and actions, and asking how they could act differently in the future.

Bob and Mona did not allow themselves to be doormats in this process. They shared their perspective so Pam and Jim could see that they weren't the only ones hurting or frustrated by the dynamics that were happening with the family.

Bob and Mona were relieved. They committed themselves to

continue working out the reconciliation with kindness, empathy, and patience. But at first they thought it was hopeless. Despite their best attempts, the dynamic remained adversarial. Pam was enraged by their attempts to listen, repent, reconcile, and forgive. On certain occasions she mocked them and called them hypocrites. She was so angry that they wondered if she might do something violent.

How do people like Mona and Bob maintain perspective and continue to work for healing when they feel defeated and attacked?

At lunch that day I suggested that Mona start by coming before the Lord to review what happened, how she herself was hurt in the experience, and then begin examining her own heart. I suggested the following questions:

- *What do I need to bring to the sacrament of confession?*
- *What do I need to forgive Jim and Pam for?*
- *If I could redo that encounter again, what would I do differently?*

After her prayerful reflection, I recommended that she go to confession and talk to a spiritual director. I reminded her that the situation would require time and space to heal, but that by God's grace it could heal.

Mona's journey gave her plenty of opportunity to practice virtue and beg the Holy Spirit to transform and empower her. She leaned on the Lord like never before. She lived what Scripture says: "If it is possible, so far as it depends on you, live peaceably with all" (Romans 12:18).

She learned to be responsible to God for her own actions despite what others were or weren't doing. She chose to act with humility and maturity. In faith she courageously chose "to do justice, and to love kindness, and to walk humbly with [her] God" (Micah 6:8) in this most difficult circumstance.

A Communion with Jesus's Passion

It is certainly dying to self when you place your desire for a restored relationship in God's hands. The pain of these situations is undoubtedly a communion with our Lord's passion. He has done everything to try to restore each of us to relationship with him. But for it truly to be a relationship of mutual love, he never forces himself upon us. He gave us a free will, and he waits patiently, continuing to send us reminders of his desire for relationship. We might push him away or ignore him. We might give him only a little of ourselves, or we might pretend to be his friend but deny knowing him in front of others. The experiences we might endure of "unrequited love" with a family member or friend is an opportunity to feel a particular aspect of Christ's passion and offer it up for the salvation of our loved ones. It's a chance to repent of what we ourselves have done to Jesus and express our regret anew.

Another woman I know, Sandra, suffered greatly because of the choices her adult son Eric was making. He rejected the faith she had raised him in, struggled with addictions, and much of the time isolated himself from the family. Sandra knew her son was not happy. The lifestyle he was living wasn't bringing him pleasure. He smoked marijuana not so much for the high as to numb the anxiety he was constantly grappling with. Sandra prayed ardently for him that he would find healing and peace from God.

God revealed to her, after years of praying for Eric, that although she prayed fervently for him, she needed to stop praying fearfully. The Lord impressed upon her the need to change the emotions she was feeling from fear to ache. She felt the Lord was telling her that the immense aching pain she was feeling out of love and longing for her son was a taste of the ache of his Sacred Heart. She was moved to have a new perspective in prayer. Her prayers were no longer desolate, anguished cries of fear; instead they were transformed into redemptive aches and tears of love united with the heart of her Saviour. She rejected fear and clung to love. "There is no fear in love, but perfect love casts out fear" (1 John 4:18).

The Saints: Our Friends in Heaven

When you have this kind of insight, you have a whole new perspective on praying devotions such as the Stations of the Cross, the sorrowful mysteries of the Rosary, the Divine Mercy Chaplet, and prayers to the Sacred Heart. Sandra no longer prays these prayers in a rote way, because in these devotions she is uniting her heart with Jesus's passion and interceding for her son. She also prays this way when she has a chance to do a Holy Hour in front of the Blessed Sacrament. She also invites the saints to join with her in her prayers for her son.

For me, the communion of saints is one of the most endearing things about joining the Catholic Church. I love the saints! I am inspired by their courage, faith, and goodness. They are role models and heroes. Fortunately they are not confined to the annals of history, or to ancient stories on library shelves. The saints make up the living body of Christ, the Church Triumphant, whereas those of us here on earth are called the Church Militant (and the souls in purgatory are referred to as the Church Suffering). The saints are alive; they are more accessible than the books we read about them. They are our friends in heaven.

Friends are awesome, especially skilled friends! When I need help with my computer, I call Cary. When I need a cake decorated, I call Hailey and Katie. When we needed help with flooring, we called Jeff. When I ask my friends for help, I know they can and will help me, because of their friendship, generosity, and talent.

I think of the saints this way. Certain saints are just the right friends for a particular need.

The kinds of situations we've been discussing here are tough. You can't force reconciliation, but you can earnestly desire it! This is when I turn to the saints for help. Of course I bring my concerns to God, too. I beg Jesus for mercy and entrust the situation to him. I turn to the Father and trust in his goodness and care of the situation. I go to the Holy Spirit, my good defense lawyer, and I ask for advice and guidance for a smooth mediation and resolution. But I also turn to the saints! I ask the saints for their intercession. I sometimes pray a nine-day novena with a particular saint. I sometimes have a conversational, "colloquy" prayer with that saint as I would with a close friend. Sometimes just reading about a saint's life gives me perspective for how I should act.

Below are some talented heavenly friends that come to mind for me. Each of these saints is amazing, and each offers so much for us as models and intercessors. The brief words I say about each of them below is just a quick taste of the amazing spiritual friendship and intercessory expertise they bring.

St. Joseph—I owe so much to St. Joseph's intercession! Our family goes to St. Joseph's Oratory at least once a year. While the kids like going to light candles in the crypt, André and I go to plead for graces in raising our children. St. Joseph has never disappointed us. I love turning to him for help since he understands our life. He was spouse, stepfather, and protector. The Church gives him many titles, but my favorite title, which I remind him of often, is "Terror of Demons." This is the kind of guy you want on your side!

St. Augustine—I love turning to St. Augustine for help when praying for young people who are caught up in worldly living and rejecting the faith of their parents.

St. Monica—In the same breath, I ask St. Monica for help, since she prayed and persevered for the conversion of her son, Augustine.

St. Paul—One of the reasons I invoke St. Paul is for reconciling relationships with co-workers (since he, Peter, John Mark, Silas, and Barnabas had "some words" and had to find a way to work things out and keep focusing on the mission).

St. John Paul II—When faced with the challenge of forgiving someone who is clearly an enemy, I think of asking St. John Paul II for prayers because he made the deliberate effort to reconcile with his imprisoned assassin.

St. Kateri—She is a beautiful young witness and intercessor for those situations when someone is mocked and rejected for his or her faith by family members.

St. André Bessette—Brother André had a very lowly position in his order. I ask him to pray for us to accept humiliation when we feel unvalued and overlooked.

St. Jude—Here's a big hitter for when you're really freaking out. He's the patron of hopeless causes. Need I say more?

St. Andrew—He is great when we are praying specifically for our siblings' salvation and our relationship with them. St. Andrew brought his brother (St. Peter) to Christ—who changed both of their lives.

St. Peter—As a leader I like to ask him to pray for me to have kindness, courage, and forgiveness when dealing with opposition from without and dissensions from within.

St. Stanislaus Kostka—A wonderful intercessor, he was persecuted and bullied by his peers, in particular his brother. His prayers for perseverance and the grace to forgive come with lived experience.

St. Francis of Assisi—Here is a saint who can pray for those who have to forgive their parents. He wanted to live completely for God and chose to reject his parents' plans for him to pursue worldly success.

St. Marguerite d'Youville—Our first Canadian-born saint knows how to pray and relate to those dealing with troubled marriages and difficult home lives. I also pray to her to help me "forgive God" for lousy situations. She never blamed God or got locked into resentment for the difficulties and setbacks she lived through.

St. Rita—This saint is a powerhouse of prayer for difficult family situations and the virtues and forgiveness needed to be faithful and loving. She, like St. Marguerite d'Youville, was a wife and a mother before becoming a religious. She is a patron saint for those suffering with marriage problems and mental illness. Along with St. Jude, she is a patron of hopeless causes.

St. Bridget of Sweden—The mother of eight, one of her children became a saint (Catherine), but several others fell away from the faith. She can help us pray for children to be reconciled to God and their family.

St. Ignatius of Loyola, St. Francis Xavier, and St. Peter Claver—These three intercessors help pray for the conversion of roommates, since they were roommates in university. St. Francis Xavier was really turned off by St. Ignatius. St. Ignatius had to seek to live at peace with him, forgive his attitudes toward him, and persevere in being good to him despite Xavier's cold reception.

Blessed Pier Giorgio Frassati—He's the cool, good-looking young man who can intercede so well for other young men. He also had to deal with opposition from his parents, so he can intercede for the kind of forgiveness needed in these relationships.

The Power of Novenas

Novenas are prayers that happen for nine days in a row. Novenas parallel the nine days the disciples waited from the time of Jesus's ascension to heaven to the promised descent of the Holy Spirit. A novena, then, is a resolute, persevering, and prayerful form of waiting. People do novenas for a particular intention, often with a particular saint in mind.

Mary, Undoer of Knots

If you are not familiar with novenas, an appropriate and powerful novena for the area of relationships is the one attributed to Mary, Undoer of Knots, sometimes called Our Lady, Undoer of Knots.

This devotion originated with a particular painting of Our Lady in St. Peter's Church in Perlack, Germany, where she is depicted as busy at work untying a rope with many knots. The artist was inspired by the words of St. Irenaeus, who built on St. Paul's teaching comparing Jesus and Adam by comparing Mary and Eve. He said: "Eve, by her disobedience, tied the knot of disgrace for the human race; whereas Mary, by her obedience, undid it."[16]

The devotion has since evolved to asking Mary for help with the knots of one's life—the complicated problems we find ourselves facing because of wrong decisions and the consequences of our sins.

In late summer 2013 I heard about Mary, Undoer of Knots, over social media. Apparently it is a favorite devotion of Pope Francis. To my surprise the next day I found a little booklet with instructions for praying a novena to Mary, Undoer of Knots, casually perched on top of a pile of books in my home office! Curious! Where did it come from? I had never seen the booklet before! I picked it up and started reading more.

I sensed the Lord was inviting me to pray this novena for a particular relationship. Over the years the way this person and I related to each other seemed to be more and more strained. I couldn't see how we could get past this way of interacting and into a healthier

---

16 St. Irenaeus, cited in "Our Lady Undoer of Knots," http://www.maryundoerofknots.com/history.htm.

place. We had tried to talk it out several times, but it never seemed to change. I didn't do just one novena to Mary, Undoer of Knots—I did at least three of them! I was counting on Mary's leadership to unravel what needed to be smoothed out.

Less than a year after discovering Our Lady, Undoer of Knots, I saw her hands at work. It was a lovely summer day, and my friend and I were sitting in my backyard. We were deep into another conversation seeking to understand one another and work things out in our relationship.

Over my friend's shoulder, in the back left-hand corner of my garden, sat our lovely white statue of Mary surrounded by flowers. As our raw, honest conversation was happening, I would glance over at Mary—quiet, still, prayerful. With the eyes of faith, it was as if I could see her listening to our conversation with her head down, slowly and calmly untying knots while we talked. I mostly listened during that three-hour conversation. Mary's intercessory presence was very consoling and strengthening to me. Even when the conversation did not seem to be going well, as I looked at the statue, I chose to trust that she knew what God was up to, that she was helping to work out the situation.

You know how it is when you're untying a knotted mess—you often have to backtrack and undo other knots to get access to the knot you were trying to work on in the first place. I chose to keep this kind of perspective by anchoring my trust in Mary's care and giving God permission to do whatever was necessary.

It also made me think of Mary's words to St. Juan Diego: "Am I not your mother?" Good moms help us untangle our messes; they take care of our problems. They somehow know how to make everything right and kiss our boo-boos. Mary is most certainly a good mom, and oh, so much more! We can turn to her for help with confidence.

In the end what transpired was the clarity to recognize that we needed space from each other. We agreed that God was opening new doors for each of us—so we could become the best versions of ourselves. I doubt that on our own we would have come to such an amicable parting of ways. We had been trying so hard to manage the difficulties that we had been blind to the possibility of other options. Even though it looked messy, Mary's nimble fingers untied the knots of our relationship so God's plan for our healing and growth could continue.

What we experienced was not unlike pruning. For greater growth and fruit to be borne, a plant's branches or blossoms must be pruned back. It seems counterintuitive, but with pruning the energy of the plant is redirected to where it can be the most productive. God prunes us, too, for our own good, as we read in the words of Jesus in John 15:

> *"I am the true vine, and my Father is the vine-grower. He removes every branch in me that bears no fruit. Every branch that bears fruit he prunes to make it bear more fruit." (John 15:1–2)*

Marriage Matters

The hub of the family is the relationship between the husband and wife. Everything that has been said about forgiveness, kindness, courage, reconciliation, mercy, and patience is practiced most frequently in the context of marriage.

Marriage as a vocation is where those of us who are spouses live as disciples. It is in this context that we pursue holiness. Holiness involves pruning, purging, and purifying. All those words tell me that there's going to be some hard work and deep cleaning going on. Husbands and wives help each other become holy—which is a pious way of saying we grate on each other!

We are perfectly designed as husband and wife to annoy each other in the very places we need to grow. It's all part of God's plan for our sanctification and perfection. My husband's weaknesses match up with my weaknesses in this delightful little way which results in conflict, irritation, and ultimately virtue development.

I get stressed out and anxious by big new projects; André thrives on new adventures. He's a starter, and I am not. I'm a finisher, and he is not. We've annoyed each other to no end. He comes home excited, announcing we should do a camping road-trip to Newfoundland. I squash his idea by reminding him that we don't have a hitch, we can't afford a camper, I'm not going to sleep in a tent, and we don't have enough time to do it. Poor guy! I'm always doing that kind of stuff to him, and he's always pulling new ideas on me. The point is more than the fact that we balance each other out; it's that we are perfecting each other. I am learning to be less impatient, unreceptive, and condescending toward others and their ideas. André is learning to think things through more and persevere in finishing.

We are growing in these specific aspects of our character fairly slowly, but we are also growing in forgiving and being patient with one another. We are learning how to live more and more at peace with each other, to respect one another, and to be honest with each other about our failings.

Marriage is our vocation and our path to holiness. We have the potential to become the best version of ourselves here, and that means being exposed to the worst of ourselves, too. It means being prepared to face all of it in each other and not recoil when the nastiness emerges. When the grating happens, instead of blaming each other, we learn to look inward. "Lord, what are you bringing out and perfecting in me through my spouse's actions?"

Marriage is not possible without forgiveness, repentance, reconciliation, and mercy. So if you're married, expect to put into practice everything I've been unpacking in this book. You can also expect to put into practice a famous passage of Scripture, which was probably the second reading at your wedding. It sounded poetic at the time, but read it now as the exhortation to mercy that it truly is:

> *Love is patient; love is kind; love is not envious or boastful or arrogant or rude. It does not insist on its own way; it is not irritable or resentful; it does not rejoice in wrongdoing, but rejoices in the truth. It bears all things, believes all things, hopes all things, endures all things. (1 Corinthians 13:4–7)*

Take just one phrase of that passage, and put it into practice, and you will go far. "Does not insist on its own way"; "is not resentful"—you name it! The New International Version says, "Love keeps no record of wrongs." I know I need to practice that! These verses are pure gold for your marriage.

Marriage should be our safe house par excellence. Although we want to avoid making mistakes, we know that if we do, it will not cause the end of everything. In marriage we strive to live in unity and peace while speaking with honesty in love.

The marriage relationship is ultimately meant to be a reflection of the relationship we have with God: a home of acceptance, mercy, and love. Both relationships make you want to become a better person.

Questions for Personal Reflection

1. *What are some formative experiences I remember which taught me how to forgive and say you're sorry?*

2. *As I read this chapter, what relationships came to mind that are a current source of tension or awkwardness?*

3. *What weaknesses did I identify in the way I am dealing with those relationships?*

4. *What perspectives and approaches resonated with me that I could apply to the strained relationships in my life?*

5. *How might I identify and unite the struggles I'm encountering in these relationships with the passion of Christ?*

6. *What devotions, spiritual practices, or saints have helped me so far on my journey? What ways is the Lord inviting me to intercede at this time in light of the situations I am currently facing?*

7. *How is the Lord forming my character through the challenges I am currently facing? What virtues is he building in me? What vices is he purging?*

—∽ **NINE** ∽—

The Body of Christ

"The eye cannot say to the hand, 'I have no need of you,' nor again the
head to the feet, 'I have no need of you.'"
—*1 Corinthians 12:21*

AS CHRISTIANS WE are not islands unto ourselves. We do not have a personal relationship with God that is exclusive. No, it is all-inclusive—we are part of the body of Christ. We do not lose ourselves in this body—we don't become anonymous contributors to a system (like in Communism or Star Trek's Borg Collective). The Catholic approach is "both/and." I have both an intimate personal relationship with God and an integral connection to everyone in the body of Christ. Love, unity, and peace is what God desires for all of us in our life together as one body, the Church.

> *As you, Father, are in me and I am in you, may they also be in us, so that the world may believe that you have sent me. The glory that you have given me I have given them, so that they may be one, as we are one, I in them and you in me, that they may become completely one, so that the world may know that you have sent me and have loved them even as you have loved me. (John 17:21–23)*

This was part of Jesus's prayer the night before his crucifixion. He prayed that we might be one, united as a people with the Triune God. I can only imagine how painful the fractions and disunity within the body of Christ are to his heart. The rifts amongst the various Christian denominations are unfortunate. Ethnic and national hostilities, abuses and hatred, are deplorable. Horrible things have been said and done by parties on every side. Even within our own denominations, dioceses, parishes, movements, ministries, and teams there are divisions and strife. It's everywhere. It cripples our witness and mission to the world. It hurts our communities and members.

At the risk of being simplistic, it boils down to unforgiveness. Remember that 90 percent of all problems are rooted in unforgiveness. As hard as this may be to accept as true in our personal life, I think we can believe it when it comes to the Christian community. Just consider a parish and all the challenges that abound with politics, bickering, gossip, and hurt people—and that's just the floral committee! Imagine how a comprehensive and sincere deep cleaning within a parish community would change things! Imagine parishes where each member chooses to release and forgive those who have hurt them so as to live in peace with God and each other.

Forgiveness and releasing is tough to sell, and tough to do in communities. It's not "feel good," "happy-clappy" messaging. It challenges us at the core of our pride and self-love.

A parish community is like a large family and includes all kinds of personalities, some of whom we don't particularly jive with. Living in peace with one another doesn't mean that we are all best friends or if we aren't enjoying being with every single person in the community, there is something wrong with us. My goodness, disagreements are not sinful per se, nor are negative feelings. Seeking peace with God and each other is rooted in a decision to live in charity and to forgive one another despite negative feelings and being conscious of disagreeing points of view. It may mean being kind and gracious when a fellow parishioner doesn't have the personal maturity or spiritual understanding to reconcile with us. Keep in mind that not all of us are working from the same rule book; each of us are wounded in our own ways which can hinder us from responding to others as we ought.

"Forgive Us Our Trespasses..."

I was astounded recently when I went to Sunday Mass in cottage country a few hours away. This parish is situated in a lovely rural community. There are many endearing things about the church, such as the Christmas lights that go around the many statues in the sanctuary (lit up year-round), and the revolving colour "disco" lights that the statue of the Sacred Heart of Jesus enjoys. Let's just say there is no lack of things to look at during Mass. What astounded me occurred when it came time to pray the Our Father. Instead of praying the prayer that Jesus taught us, we sang a song, which took certain artistic liberties. Whoever composed it combined his or her own lyrics with the words of the Our Father. The curious thing, though, was that one sentence was missing—only one. "Forgive us our trespasses, as we forgive those who trespass against us" wasn't there.

> *Our Father who art in heaven, hallowed by thy name. Thy kingdom come; thy will be done, on earth as it is in heaven. Give us this day our daily bread, and lead us not into temptation, but deliver us from evil. Amen.*

Interesting, isn't it? The Our Father sounds very safe without that one line. Now it's a feel-good prayer. I'm sure the song's composer thought so, too. "If I take out this unfortunate line about trespasses, I could make a really pleasant song out of the Our Father!"

But this line is what these parishioners need to hear, pray, and do. Their souls depend on it. The Our Father is not a poem; it is truth, and the body of Christ needs to live it. Every parish I've ever been in is dripping with conflicts and complaints, and I dare to say that the majority of the time they are not ideologically based—they are personality-based. Resentments have a long, convoluted history, and like an invasive weed, they run far, deep, and wide. Church gossip is a cancer in our communities. Pope Francis addressed the issue of gossip at the Sunday Angelus on February 16, 2014:[17]

---

17 Pope Francis, Sunday Angelus, February 16, 2014, quoted in Kerri Lenartowick, "Gossip Is Poisonous, Insists Pope," Catholic News Agency, February 16, 2014, http://www.catholicnewsagency.com/news/gossip-is-poisonous-insists-pope.

It's so rotten, gossip. At the beginning, it seems to be something enjoyable and fun, like a piece of candy. But at the end, it fills the heart with bitterness and also poisons us.... I tell you the truth, I am convinced that if each one of us would purposely avoid gossip, at the end, we would become a saint! It's a beautiful path!

His message was on the topic of proper relationships in our communities. He talked about the demand for forgiveness found in the Our Father and the challenge to reconcile with our brothers and sisters in the faith as taught in St. Matthew's Gospel:

So when you are offering your gift at the altar, if you remember that your brother or sister has something against you, leave your gift there before the altar and go; first be reconciled to your brother or sister, and then come and offer your gift. (Matthew 5:23–24)

This passage challenges us to take the high ground and approach someone who might have a problem with us. When I think about this passage, I wonder how many of us have gone to Mass unreconciled with a brother or sister in Christ. I actually think about that passage at every Mass when we exchange the peace of Christ. The collection basket has gone around, and we put money in it. The bread and wine were brought up from the congregation as we sang and prayed the offertory songs and prayers. Jesus is on the altar—literally as the gift and sacrifice for our redemption individually and as a people. We pray the Our Father next, confessing that we are one family, and with our "Amen" we confirm Christ's weighty prayer, "Forgive us our trespasses, as we forgive those who trespass against us."

And then just before we all receive his Body and Blood together as a community, we interrupt the flow of the liturgy in order to offer one another the peace of Christ. This isn't a welcoming gimmick the hospitality team came up with! It is an opportunity to fulfill Jesus's desire that we are at peace with our brothers and sisters. Offering each other the sign of peace directly after we've prayed the Our

Father is a concrete response to the words "we forgive those who trespass against us."

Wouldn't it be beautiful if the disposition of our heart when offering each other the peace of Christ communicated "I hope you can forgive me for what I did"? And if the "Peace of Christ" said in reply was understood to mean, "Be at peace, my brother, my sister. Jesus Christ forgave me so I could have peace with God; I will do no less with you"?

I'm sure it happens, but I don't think it happens too often. Frankly, even the opposite happens. Someone recently told me about her experience at the sign of peace. Earlier that week she had found herself in a conflict with one of the liturgical committee members. She tried her best to resolve things, but the head of that committee was too insulted to talk about it. As it turned out they ended up sitting two people apart at Mass that Sunday. My friend turned, leaned forward, and looked straight at the other woman to offer her the peace of Christ. And for the record, she actually meant what she was offering. But the other lady ignored my friend's body language. She resolutely stood there, staring straight ahead so as not to catch her eye. No, the peace of Christ didn't happen here.

How often does it really happen well? It's usually a nice little interaction with folks sitting nearby. There are some handshakes, and touching embraces amongst family members: a kiss, a hug. Occasionally there are those awkward exchanges with strangers.

"So, are we shaking hands here or not? Oh, I see; we're just nodding to each other. Well, at least you're looking me in the eyes now."

In my case the sign of peace is a little wake-up call from my daydreaming. "Pay attention, it's almost time to walk up for Communion." Pathetic, I know.

The Peace of Christ

Gerry, an older man in our parish, is very friendly and feels very comfortable around our family. He was evidently so comfortable that he felt he could give us unsolicited feedback and advice. One particular Sunday I received a phone call from him at two in the afternoon.

"Hello, Angèle; it was nice to see you and the family at Mass today."

"Thank you, Gerry; it was nice to see you, too."

"You know, I couldn't help but notice some of the children's interactions. I have studied childhood development, and I thought you should know that I see some things I'm concerned about."

My mind quickly raced back in time and fast-forwarded through how the kids had behaved during the Mass. My overview looked pretty good—there had been no screaming, no exploding Cheerio containers, no bickering. On the contrary, I recalled how the older children had lovingly cared for the younger ones. From my vantage point it was a "family Mass win," so what could he mean?

He proceeded to tell me that our three-year-old was clearly spoiled because all the older children were constantly caring for her and keeping her happy in the pew, and that this would surely lead to serious developmental issues.

I couldn't believe it. "I'm flabbergasted that felt you had to phone me to say something like this about our parenting! The children were wonderfully behaved at Mass—you saw that. The older kids aren't spoiling their little sister; they are just delighting in her and caring for her. And besides, she's only three years old! The only good thing about this call is that I'm glad you're doing it to me. Please never do this to anyone else."

The next Sunday as I walked in through the parish doors, it felt like my heart was beating outside of my chest. I could hear the words of Christ in my head:

> *So when you are offering your gift at the altar, if you remember that your brother or sister has something against you, leave your gift there before the altar and go; first be reconciled to your brother or sister, and then come and offer your gift.*

I'm so angry with Gerry. I don't think I can receive the Eucharist today if I don't make peace with him. I don't what I'll do if I see him. I might punch him in the face if I see him. Maybe I can manage to avoid him, and this will all fade away with time. My eyes scanned the sanctuary to see where he might be sitting. The coast was clear. We sat in our pew, and I focused on calming down. As we stood up to sing the entrance hymn, however, there he was, across from us on the other side of the church.

All through Mass I wrestled with my thoughts and emotions toward him. What should I do? What did God want me to do? I was offended by his words, but I had forgiven him. Yet I was still dealing my anger and emotions, and I needed to make peace with God and with Gerry. As Mass went on and the sign of peace inched closer, I knew what the Lord was telling me to do. He was telling me to make peace with my brother before I went to the altar.

So when Father said, "Let us offer each other the sign of peace," I swallowed my pride, slipped out of the pew, walked over to Gerry, extended my hand, looked him in the eye, and said, "Peace of Christ." In turn he replied, "Peace of Christ," and shook my hand. That was it. It was enough. We were at peace.

It looked like any other exchange of the peace of Christ, other than the fact that I walked halfway across the church to give it. André, knowing the story, was amazed that I shook Gerry's hand. I suppose I shouldn't be surprised that I went back to my pew feeling tremendous peace. St. Ignatius of Loyola said:

> *The peace of our Lord is something interior, and it brings with it all the other gifts and graces necessary for salvation and eternal life. This peace makes us love our neighbor for the love of our Creator and Lord, and because of this same love we observe all the commandments of the law, as St. Paul says: "He who loves his neighbor has fulfilled the law" (Romans 13:8). He has fulfilled the law because he loves his Creator and Lord and loves his neighbor for his Lord's sake.*[18]

The incident with Gerry wasn't the first time he had offended me, and I'm pretty sure it won't be the last. But that's what parish and community life is like. We are God's family. You don't pick your family; you learn to love them, understand them, be patient with

---

18 St. Ignatius of Loyola, *Monumenta Ignatiana: Epistolae et Instructiones*, vol. 12 (Madrid, 1903–1911), 1:162.

them, confront them as necessary, and always be good to them, even when they are driving you crazy.

Striving to live in peace might mean we need to embrace Ephesians 4:15 by "speaking the truth in love." It involves the hard work of talking things through.

Sometimes striving to live in peace means that the Lord is asking us to bear with others in the midst of experiencing negative feelings. We don't have to suppress our feelings of frustration—those are normal reactions. We can take them in stride and not feel guilty about them, but we also need to take those feelings to prayerful discernment.

We can ask, "Lord, what are you asking me to do about this situation out of love for you and this brother or sister?" He might be asking us to patiently put up with the situation, forgive them in our hearts, and love them despite the lack of kindness we receive in return. We might not feel love oozing out of our pores toward them, but in obedience to God we can choose to be good and wish good for them despite the circumstances. In some instances the Lord might answer the question by saying, "Out of my love for you, I want you to remove yourself from the situation because this relationship is not healthy for you."

Ultimately it is a discernment of what love requires; whether the loving action is speaking the truth in love and actively seeking reconciliation, or whether it is being patient and loving people where they are.

In this book I can't presume to propose a comprehensive solution to the rifts and divisions in our parishes, movements, ministries, and teams. However, I can offer a few tips as a starting point.

Self-Examination

Always start with yourself. Take the situation to prayer and examine yourself in the light of Christ's law.

- *How did I fail to love?*
- *How did I seek to hurt the other?*
- *How did I inadvertently hurt the other?*

- *What is my role in this situation?*
- *What could I have done differently?*
- *What do I need to confess to the person and to God?*
- *What next steps is the Lord asking me to do in this situation and in this relationship?*
- *When can I get to confession?*
- *Should I talk to a spiritual director about this?*

Reaching Out

Through your prayerful self-reflection or advice from a priest in confession, you probably have a plan to reach out and seek reconciliation. Here are some tips:

Invite. You can't force someone to reconcile, but you can make the first move. You might need to give the other person some space to calm down and agree to get together with you. A brief e-mail, letter, or text saying you would like to talk things over is an acceptable medium. Although it's not as effective as face-to-face communication, it does give the person freedom to process the request without you standing there, staring at him or her.

The written word, void of tone and body language, can cause much misinterpretation. I certainly advise against trying to reconcile via e-mail. It's very tempting because it avoids conflict, but it also can create more conflict and confusion. If you do write an e-mail, it's beneficial to have someone else read it before you hit "send" to make sure nothing could come across the wrong way.

If you receive an e-mail that seems to be written with a snarky tone, refrain from judgment. Give the other person the benefit of the doubt. Maybe he or she wrote you in distress, or too quickly or without reviewing it; maybe the way it sounds to you is not really what the other person was meaning to convey. Keep in mind that your own insecurities and issues form a lens that skews your perception of reality.

If the person agrees to meet with you, I recommend going somewhere neutral, such as a coffee shop. You'll be in public, so you'll be more inclined to behave civilly—and a cup of coffee and a treat softens the mood, especially when you're buying.

And of course, pray! Pray for protection during the conversation. Give God permission to do whatever he needs to do in this situation. Pray that the Holy Spirit will prepare both of your hearts for reconciliation. Invite your heavenly friends and, if appropriate, a trusted earthly friend or two to intercede for this meeting.

Listen. When you get together, put the other person first and give him or her the first chance to speak. Maybe just meeting you is a huge step for the person and you'll need to take the initiative to get the conversation going. Besides, you called the meeting, so you can start it.

Let the person know your intention—that you want to make peace with him or her, you want to hear his or her side of the story, and you want to explain where you are coming from.

Practice good listening skills and empathy; seek to understand and use the mirroring technique to say back to the person what you hear so that it's clear that you truly understand his or her point of view. Aim to speak with kindness.

Be Prepared. Be prepared to apologize for what you've done or failed to do. Maybe as you listen to the person, you realize some things you need to apologize for. Verbalize and admit your failures.

You've got something to say too, though! You've also been hurt. Be prepared to communicate what you need so the other person hears your point of view, but whatever you do, do not come to the meeting with a list on a clipboard! Prepare well and trust that the Holy Spirit will bring to mind exactly what you should say.

I have found it helpful to frame what I need to say as a three-part assertion message. Assertiveness (not aggression) is another way of explaining Cinderella's brand of courage. Being assertive is choosing to communicate the truth in love.

A three-part assertion message is a tool that allows you to communicate clearly and concisely what someone is doing and how that affects you. Just building your three-part assertion message is an effective way to sift through a situation and narrow it down to the fundamental behaviours. This method empowers you to distill your message into one clear and brief sentence.

When you _____,
(state the behaviour clearly, objectively, and nonjudgmentally)
*I feel*_____,
(describe your feelings)
*because*_____.
(identify the tangible effect on your life)

It is very important to be emotionally neutral in your choice of words. This is no time for exaggeration, coarse language, or accusations. Here's what a three-part assertion message might look like:

When you roll your eyes while I am talking in a meeting, I feel disrespected, because your body language communicates to me and everyone else in the room that what I have to say doesn't matter.

When you make decisions without consulting me, I feel frustrated because I have to execute the plan, but I do not understand the logic behind your decisions.

Taking the time to thoughtfully build a true three-part assertion message is a huge asset in your attempts to communicate and reconcile.

Wrap Up. After the conversation, assuming it has gone fairly well, here are some steps to wrap things up. Review what was apologized for and express your thanks for what the other person communicated.

Here are some great follow-up questions.

"Are we good?" This helps establish if there is anything unfinished that should be discussed now (or at another time).

"What can I do to handle this better next time?" This is an excellent question to help you understand how to improve, and it gives the one questioned a chance to express his or her needs and feel heard.

Close with a brief prayer of thanksgiving to God. Even if you're in a public place, you can do this subtly.

Seek Mediation. If the conversation didn't lead to peace, pull back and evaluate what happened. Again start with the way you handled things. Speak to a trusted friend, spiritual director, or priest to get advice for next steps. They might suggest involving a third party for mediation, and this is scriptural.

> *If another member of the church sins against you, go and point out the fault when the two of you are alone. If the member listens to you, you have regained that one. But if you are not listened to, take one or two others along with you, so that every word may be confirmed by the evidence of two or three witnesses. If the member refuses to listen to them, tell it to the church. (Matthew 18:15–17)*

No one wants to get into scenarios that involve mediation and confrontation. If we all kept close tabs on our own hearts and weeded out resentments as soon as they appear, the body of Christ would be a peaceful experience.

Be Proactive—Plan Ahead

When it comes to reconciliation, be proactive and consider what you will do the next time you're insulted, frustrated, hurt, miffed, or defied.

My first line of defense is a good defense lawyer. Invoke the Holy Spirit right away to give you counsel and guide your responses. Pray that he will reveal to you what you should do in that moment and empower you to do it. Ask the Holy Spirit the classic question, "WWJD [What would Jesus do]?" Ask him, "How am I supposed to respond to this situation right now?" Ask Mother Mary to pray that you will have the grace to "do whatever he tells you" (John 2:5).

Next time, from past situations remember the areas that require improvement. Be mindful of your weaknesses and ask for the grace to practice better ways of relating with people.

And finally, the next time you're in a conflict, remember Cinderella. Remember kindness and courage. Act with kindness and stand with courage. Be careful not to let your courage come from defensiveness, pride, or vengeance. Christian courage is not a reaction—it is the result of who we are in God. It comes from our principal foundation—the deep knowing that we are loved and cherished as a child of God anchors us during stormy conflicts.

The difficulty to live in unity as brothers and sisters in the family of God is all around us. It's overwhelming, and it's a disgrace. What comes to mind right now is a line from a classic church song, "Let there be peace on earth, and let it begin with me." That's what it boils down to, isn't it? I need to keep tabs on my own heart and judgments toward others in the body of Christ. I need to take the initiative to reconcile. I need to resist the temptation to enter into gossip. I need to strive to live at peace with all.

> As God's chosen ones, holy and beloved, clothe yourselves with compassion, kindness, humility, meekness, and patience. Bear with one another and, if anyone has a complaint against another, forgive each other; just as the Lord has forgiven you, so you also must forgive. Above all, clothe yourselves with love, which binds everything together in perfect harmony. And let the peace of Christ rule in your hearts, to which indeed you were called in the one body. (Colossians 3:12–15)

Questions for Personal Reflection

1. Where is there discord in my particular Christian communities?

2. How am I contributing to the conflicts?

3. How can I combat the poison of gossip?

4. Is there anyone I need to repent to in my Christian communities?

5. Is there anyone who has a problem with me?

6. Do I have a problem with someone that should be addressed? (I will prepare a three-part assertion message to communicate these concerns.)

7. What could I do better in the future when I experience conflict with someone in my Christian community?

8. What could I do better in the future when trying to resolve conflicts with someone?

9. Is there something the Lord is inviting me to do to facilitate reconciliation in the broader body of Christ?

━ ∞ TEN ∞ ━

Ultimate Mercy

"For God so loved the world that he gave his only Son, so that everyone who believes in him may not perish but may have eternal life."
—John 3:16

TO MAKE SURE he was good and dead—in order to "get it over with" before the Sabbath—the Roman soldier pierced the side of Jesus, and blood and water sprayed forth. This is the original experience of Divine Mercy—he willingly laid down his life so we would no longer be subject to the wages of sin: death and separation from God. Christ's death and resurrection brought us the possibility and hope of new life.

This is the basic gospel message. Jesus made a way for us so we could have peace with God again. He atoned for our sins, and he offers us a new life and a fresh start as a free gift. Through faith and the waters of baptism, we receive his mercy. It is his gift to us—a gift we do not deserve and could never earn. It's more than we could imagine.

When you read this, what is going on in your head? I understand if you're thinking, *Yep, sure, I get it. Heard it before. Next.* This is where my journey started. The message of the gospel was so familiar to me that I was practically numb to it. I believed it, and I knew it was a message I was supposed to proclaim to the world, but I didn't really think it was a message I personally needed to hear.

But now when I share the Good News, it's different. It's no longer merely a Bible story or a cliché. *It's my love story.* I was hurt, pathetic, afraid, and weak. I was critical, mean, angry, and bitter. I was self-satisfied, proud, arrogant, and blind. But Jesus broke through all of it. He died to rescue me from myself, and he loved me enough to make sure I really understood what he had done for me.

I love how St. Augustine describes the way God invaded his life and unveiled the truth.

> *Late have I loved you, O Beauty ever ancient, ever new, late have I loved you! You were within me, but I was outside, and it was there that I searched for you. In my unloveliness I plunged into the lovely things which you created. You were with me, but I was not with you. Created things kept me from you; yet if they had not been in you they would not have been at all. You called, you shouted, and you broke through my deafness. You flashed, you shone, and you dispelled my blindness. You breathed your fragrance on me; I drew in breath and now I pant for you. I have tasted you, now I hunger and thirst for more. You touched me, and I burned for your peace.*[19]

Although my life is very different from St. Augustine's, in my own way I, too, was trapped in serious sin and oblivious to the matter. I thought I was doing great and God was lucky to have me on his side. I was clueless. Even though I had heard it all before, the words of truth did not penetrate my thick skull. Thank God, he broke through my blindness and revealed the gravity of my sin to me. He showed me that my judgments, dishonouring my parents, and my deliberate (and self-justified) refusal to forgive put my salvation in jeopardy.

This is my prayer for this book. My goal is to share the message I desperately needed to "get"—that forgiveness matters and unforgiveness condemns. We will never receive mercy for nothing. The Lord is very clear on this point. He spoke often, purposefully, and emphatically that we must forgive and show mercy if we wish to receive it from God. He tells us we have to forgive everyone, without

---

19 St. Augustine, *Confessions*, book X, cited in Sacred-Texts.com, http://www.sacred-texts.com/chr/augconf/aug10.htm.

exception. We have to forgive always, without limit. This is a hard teaching, and it has eternal consequences. Jesus was very clear about it, and he used the drama of stories and parables to emphasise that forgiving others from your heart really matters.

Forgiveness matters! For the love of God and the hope of heaven, embrace and choose forgiveness.

Obeying the call to forgiveness doesn't mean God won and you lost; forgiveness is the key to your freedom. It is the key we've been given to unlock our prison cell.

Do yourself a favour and step out of the shadows of your prison cell, unlock the door, and step out into the light and freedom forgiveness brings. When you open that door, God then asks you to open another door—the door of your heart—so he can come in.

Listen! I am standing at the door, knocking; if you hear my voice and open the door, I will come in to you and eat with you, and you with me. (Revelation 3:20)

So what will you do?

Let him in! You can pray a prayer like this one:

Father, I believe that you know me and love me. I have not always chosen to love you, and I have broken my relationship with you through my sins. Thank you for sending your Son, Jesus, who proved your love for me on the cross. Lord Jesus, I open the door of my heart and invite you to be at the centre of my life—to be my Saviour and my Lord. Direct me by your Holy Spirit and help me to live the gospel with my whole life. Amen.

Sometimes people are afraid to pray a prayer like that, but you've come so far now with all this talk about forgiveness and repentance—how could you withhold your heart from him? How could you be afraid?

If we let Christ into our lives, we lose nothing, nothing, absolutely nothing, of what makes life free, beautiful, and great.

No! Only in this friendship are the doors of life opened wide. Only in this friendship is the great potential of human existence truly revealed.... Do not be afraid of Christ! He takes nothing away and he gives you everything. When we give ourselves to him, we receive a hundredfold in return. Yes, open, open wide the doors to Christ—and you will find true life.[20]

Questions for Personal Reflection

1. Am I convinced that Jesus died on the cross to save me from my sins and restore me to relationship with God? Am I grateful for this?

2. How do I know that forgiveness matters?

3. Am I ready to truly walk out of the prison of unforgiveness? What is the Lord asking me to do in this regard?

4. Have I opened the door of my heart and invited God to be at the centre of my life? Is there anything preventing me from doing that?

---

20 Benedict XVI, Homily at St. Peter's Square, April 24, 2005, https://w2.vatican.va/content/benedict-xvi/en/homilies/2005/documents/hf_ben-xvi_hom_20050424_inizio-pontificato.html.

⸺ ✂ APPENDIX ✂ ⸺
The Forgiveness Prayer

The following prayer, written by Fr. Robert DeGrandis, SSJ, and used with his permission, may be a useful resource for you as you work through forgiveness. Not all parts of the prayer apply to everyone, but it is a model that you can use, and it includes people in your life you may not have realized you needed to forgive.

LORD JESUS CHRIST, I ask today to forgive everyone in my life. I know that you will give me strength to forgive, and I thank you that you love me more than I love myself and want my happiness more than I desire it for myself.

Lord Jesus, I want to be free from the feelings of resentment, bitterness, and unforgiveness toward you for the times I thought you sent death, hardships, financial difficulties, punishments, and sickness into our family.

Lord, I forgive myself for my sins, faults, and failings. For all that is truly bad in myself or all that I think is bad, I do forgive myself. For any delving into the occult, Ouija boards, horoscopes, séances, fortune telling, lucky charms; for taking your name in vain; for not worshipping you; for hurting my parents, for getting drunk; for taking dope; for sins against my purity; for adultery; for abortion; for stealing, for lying—I am truly forgiving myself today. Thank you, Lord, for your grace at this moment.

I truly forgive my mother. I forgive her for all the times she hurt me, resented me, was angry with me, and for all the times she preferred my brothers and sisters to me. I forgive her for the times she told me I was dumb, ugly, stupid, the worst of the children, or that I cost the family a lot of money. For the times she told me I was unwanted, an accident, a mistake, or not what she expected, I forgive her.

I forgive my father. I forgive him for any nonsupport, any lack of love, affection, or attention. I forgive him for any lack of time, for not giving me his companionship, for his drinking or arguing and fighting with my mother or the other children. For his severe punishments, for desertion, for being away from home, for divorcing my mother, or for any running around, I do forgive him.

Lord, I extend forgiveness to my sisters and brothers. I forgive those who rejected me, lied about me, hated me, resented me, competed for my parents' love; those who hurt me, who physically harmed me. For those who were too severe on me, punished me, or made my life unpleasant in any way, I do forgive them.

Lord, I forgive my spouse for lack of love, attention, support, warmth, understanding; his or her bad habits, falling away from the Church; any bad actions which disturb me.

My God, I forgive my in-laws—mother, father, son or daughter-in-law, sister or brother-in-law, and other relatives by marriage. For their lack of love, words of criticism, thoughts, actions, or omissions, which injure and cause pain, I do forgive them.

Please help me to forgive my relatives and grandparents who may have interfered in our family, been possessive of my parents, may have caused confusion, or turned one parent against the other.

Jesus, help me to forgive my co-workers who are disagreeable or make life miserable for me. For those who push their work off on me, gossip about me, won't cooperate with me, try to take my job, I do forgive them.

My neighbors need to be forgiven, Lord. For all their noise, letting their property run down, not tying up their dogs who run through my yard, not taking in their trash cans, being prejudiced, and running down the neighborhood, I do forgive them.

I now forgive my clergyman, my congregation, and my church for all their lack of support, pettiness, bad sermons, lack of friendliness, not affirming me as they should, not providing me with inspiration, for not using me in a key position, for not inviting me to serve in a major capacity, and for any other hurt they have inflicted—I do forgive them today.

Lord, I forgive all professional people who have hurt me in any way—doctors, nurses, lawyers, policemen, hospital workers. For anything that they did to me, I truly forgive them today.

Lord, I forgive my employer for not paying me enough money, for not appreciating my work, for being unkind and unreasonable with me, for being angry or unfriendly, for not promoting me, and for not complimenting me on my work.

Lord, I forgive my schoolteachers and instructors of the past, as well as the present. For those who punished me, humiliated me, insulted me, treated me unjustly, made fun of me, called me dumb or stupid, made me stay after school.

Lord, I forgive my friends who have let me down, lost contact with me, do not support me, were not available when I needed help, borrowed money and did not return it, gossiped about me.

Lord Jesus, I especially pray for the grace of forgiveness for that one person in life who has hurt me the most. I ask to forgive anyone who I consider my greatest enemy, the one who is the hardest to forgive, or the one who I said I would never forgive.

Thank You, Jesus, that I am free of the evil of unforgiveness. Let your Holy Spirit fill me with light, and let every dark area of my mind be enlightened. Amen.

—⌒ ABOUT THE AUTHOR ⌒—

ANGÈLE REGNIER IS co-founder, along with her husband André, of Catholic Christian Outreach. Catholic Christian Outreach (CCO) is a university student movement that has been engaged in the new evangelization for over twenty-five years. Angèle and André received the Pro Ecclesia et Pontifice Medal, given for distinguished service to the Church and the highest medal awarded to the laity by the Pope.

Angèle is a convert to the Catholic faith. Raised in a Lutheran and Evangelical church background, she became a Roman Catholic in 1988. She played a leading role in developing CCO's methodology and writing the five books of their small-group faith study series. These materials have been translated into many languages and are being used on campuses and in parishes around the world.

Angèle is a natural teacher and an entertaining speaker who shares her passion for the saints, the "Great Commission," and abandonment to God's will. She is also a spiritual director with a focus on Ignatian spirituality.

She is the mother of five hilarious kids and the proud grandmother of one. The Regniers currently reside in Ottawa, Ontario, Canada, but still consider Saskatchewan to be "home."